CW00418779

PESAḤ

Insights from the Past, Present, and Future

The Shlomo Kalati Edition

PESAḤ
Insights from the Past, Present, and Future
The Shlomo Kalati Edition

First Edition, 2022

ISBN:
Paperback: 9798404363463
Hardback: 9798791143860

www.TheHabura.com

Typeset by Avner Yeshurun
+1 305-761-3561
ayeshurun@gmail.com

THE
ḤABURA

www.TheHabura.com

✦

the SEPHARDI community

Montefiore Endowment

DANGOOR EDUCATION

THE SENIOR RABBI'S OFFICE

ויתן אלהים חכמה לשלמה ותבונה הרבה מאד ורחב לב כחול אשר על שפת הים

God endowed Solomon with wisdom and discernment in great measure, with understanding as vast as the sands on the seashore. [I Kings 5:9]

✦

In loving memory of

SHLOMO KALATI *z"l*

Cherished Husband and Beloved Father

For whom Passover was another opportunity for loving kindness and for whom כל דכפין ייתי ויכול was a way of life.

✦

לעילוי נשמת
בעלי האהוב ומו׳ר אבינו

שלמה בן אליהו ודינה כלאתי ז״ל

נלב״ע ו׳ תמוז תשפ״א
ת.נ.צ.ב.ה

Dedicated in honour of Rosh Bet Midrash Rabbi Joseph Dweck, Sina Kahen, and all those involved in supporting The Ḥabura.

In great appreciation for the approach in Torah being shared and developed.

May they see continued strength in this unique and important initiative.

Moshe & Raquel Laniado

What is The Ḥabura?

The Ḥabura is an online and global *Bet Midrash* dedicated to studying, teaching, and publishing Torah as a lens through which we view and interact with God's world. This approach is rooted in, but not exclusive to, the classical Sephardi *mesora* that we uphold and cherish.

Since our inception in 2020, we have grown to teach hundreds of international students from across four continents and who work in a variety of professions. We have been honoured to host *Dayanim*, *Rabbanim*, and leading experts from around the world to teach us *Miqra*, *Halakha*, *Talmud*, *Maḥshaba*, and History.

Under the guidance of our *Rosh Bet Midrash*, Rabbi Joseph Dweck, and with the assistance of the S&P Sephardi Community of the UK, the Montefiore Endowment, and Dangoor Education, The Ḥabura has been able to utilise the latest technologies to teach and publish authentic, cutting-edge, and relevant Torah-study materials to an unlimited and ever-growing number of Jews, wherever they may live.

For information about our online curriculum, publishing house and more, please visit **www.TheHabura.com.**

✦

CONTENTS

✦

Introduction

Senior Rabbi Joseph Dweck

Rabbi Joseph Dweck is the Senior Rabbi of the S&P Sephardi Community of the UK – the country's oldest Jewish community. He is also the Rosh Bet Midrash of The Ḥabura. He studied in Jerusalem at Yeshivat Hazon Ovadia under the tutelage of the former Sephardi Chief Rabbi of Israel, Rabbi Ovadia Yosef. He has an MA in Jewish education. In his capacity as Senior Rabbi, Rabbi Dweck serves as a President of the Council of Christians and Jews, Deputy President of the London School of Jewish Studies, Ecclesiastical Authority of the Board of Deputies of British Jews, and Standing Committee Member of the Conference of European Rabbis. Visit www.SeniorRabbi.com to find out more about his work and initiatives.

The festival of Pesaḥ does not only commemorate the historic liberation of our ancestors from slavery in ancient Egypt. It is also designed to engage us in thought, speech, and behaviour that encourages and guides us to living lives of freedom.

A major aspect of freedom that Pesaḥ addresses is the mental component. It is in our ability to be the masters of our own minds and choose our best options for a life that is healthy, whole and successful that we are truly free. Almost everything we experience is the product of human thought. The cities, homes, countries in which we live; science, medicine, art, music; all of these come from human thinking. How we understand and perceive the phenomena of our everyday experiences is the greatest determinant of the quality of our lives. The more we understand about the nature of freedom, the more we are able to act as free people.

One act that guides our consciousness on Pesaḥ is that we fulfill a command to tell our story. One reason we do this is in order to orient ourselves towards the events and people that formed us as a nation and thereby, to better know our identity. In doing so we also become sensitive to sequence and consequence which in turn informs our choices. We illuminate it with insight, conceptual analysis, and meaningful commentary so we can better understand ourselves and the world. For it is by this that we come to know how best to live our lives.

In these pages, both teachers and students of our virtual Bet Midrash - The Ḥabura - engage in the age-old endeavour of thought on Pesaḥ, its story, its lessons and its components so that we all might benefit from the ideas that are derived and presented. We are especially excited to include in this edition essays from Ḥakham Ben Zion Uziel *z"l* (1880-1953), former Sephardi Chief Rabbi of Israel, as well as my predecessor, Ḥakham Benjamin Artom *z"l* (1835-1879). I hope that this volume will serve as an inspirational companion to this beautiful festival.

I wish to thank all those who contributed for their time, effort and dedication. Many thanks to Nachman Davies for painstakingly editing the text, and to Avner Yeshurun for typesetting it. And great thanks to Sina Kahen, Avi Garson, and Eli Shaubi for their undying dedication in ensuring that The Ḥabura and all of its exciting projects are active and successful. May they all be blessed according to their investments.

Wishing you all a *Ḥag Kasher VeSameaḥ!*

Joseph Dweck
Rosh Bet Midrash
Senior Rabbi, S&P Sephardi Community

✦

Insights from the Past

The Knowledge of God

Ḥakham Benjamin Artom

Ḥakham Benjamin Artom (1835-1879) was the Chief Rabbi of the Spanish & Portuguese community – the oldest Rabbinic office, and the oldest Jewish community, in the United Kingdom. He was born in Asti, Piedmont, Italy in 1835. Soon after, his father, Elia, passed away and Rabbi Artom's maternal uncle then assumed his brother-in-law's parental responsibilities. Rabbi Artom held multiple rabbinical positions throughout Italy and taught many languages including Hebrew, Italian, French, and German. Rabbi Artom was the first rabbi to hold office in Naples, Italy.

In 1866 Rabbi Artom moved to London, to become the Ḥakham of the Spanish and Portuguese Jews' Congregation. The Rabbi arrived in England knowing only basic English, so he would deliver his first sermons in French. However, a year later, the Ḥakham's command of the English language was so great that his sermons were delivered with a unique eloquence and were later compiled into a book in the year 1873. Some 15 years after the Rabbi's arrival, many of the synagogues in London were considering amalgamation under the leadership of the Ashkenazi Chief Rabbi, Nathan Marcus Adler.

Rabbi Artom managed to resist such pressure and maintain the independence of his Sephardi community while maintaining good relations with the Ashkenazim.

The Ḥakham approved and supported the construction of many other Sephardi synagogues (such as the Dutch Synagogue in London, and the first Sephardi Synagogue in Manchester) even after the Ashkenazi Chief Rabbi had denied such approval. In 1877, the Ḥakham agreed to accept converts into the Sephardi community in England. Ḥakham Artom was loyal to the tradition and worked towards unifying the various sects of Judaism that were emerging in his time. Rabbi Artom held his position as the Ḥakham of the Spanish and Portuguese Jews' Congregation in England until his passing in 1879.

The following essay, "The Knowledge of God," is from Rabbi Artom's *Book of Sermons*, published in London in 1873.

✦

"וידעתם כי אני יי אלהיכם"

"And ye shall know that I am the Lord your God."

Exodus 16:7

שאל פרעה למשה ולאהרן מי ה׳ אמרו לו אלהינו הוא אלהים חיים ומלך עולם. אמר להם כמה שנותיו כמה עיירות כבש אמר לו אלהינו כחו וגבורתו מלא עולם וכו׳:

'Who is your god?' said Pharaoh unto Moses and Aaron. 'Our God is the living God, and the King of the universe.' 'How old is He? What has He achieved? How many cities has He conquered?' 'Our God fills the universe with His power, He existed before the creation of the world, and will exist when the world shall end; He created thee, and breathed into thee the breath of life.'

Midrash Shemot Rabba, ch. 5

✦

There are few events in the whole Bible as highly important as the oppression, the rising and the deliverance of a whole nation, as well as the obduracy and the exemplary punishment of all its tormentors: of the king, his ministers, his people, and even the land in which tyranny had been pitilessly exercised. Throughout the history of ancient nations, there are few narratives that possess the characteristics of impressiveness and interest, which are as dramatic as that contained in the first four sections of Exodus. Yet infinitely more significant are the moral lessons which we may derive from each phase of that startling event, from each page and each line of that wonderful narration. From them, we may deduce religious and moral improvement, and it becomes our sacred duty to master them by constant study and untiring reflection. For this object alone it was said: "This book of the Law shall not depart out of thy mouth, but thou shalt meditate therein day and night."[1] For this object alone wherever there has been a Jew, during two thousand years, a section of the Pentateuch has been read every Sabbath with solemnity and devotion. Let us now briefly dwell upon the most salient principle to be learnt from the chapters which we have read this morning, and which can be summarised by these words: *the knowledge of God.*

God created man in His own image, and from that man whom He made out of the dust, and whom He animated by an immortal spirit, from that source alone descended all mankind. Of this great truth, proclaimed in the very first pages of the Law, we are often reminded, so that men reflecting upon the oneness of their origin may learn to love each other. No one human family can claim to spring from a nobler source than another; and no nation can have the right of enslaving another nation. Slavery is an insult to that Providence which made all human races equal to each other, whatever the physical modifications may be to which they have been subjected by the influence of climate. When therefore the Egyptians, trampling upon all the laws of justice and hospitality, turned into slaves those whom they had willingly received as guests, when they treated them barbarously, and not content with condemning them to the hardest labour, attempted to prevent their increase by throwing those unfortunate little beings into the depths of the Nile, whose only crime was to be of Jewish parentage, then the wrath of the Lord broke forth, then He stretched out His arm and lifted His hand, in order to punish those who had refused to believe in His

1 Joshua 1:8

existence and acknowledge His power, and who had rejected His command to give liberty to the race which He had chosen; in order to punish those who had dared to say: "Who is the Eternal, whose voice I am to obey to let Israel go? I know not the Eternal, nor will I let Israel go."[2]

We know the ten plagues which infected the elements and which arose in terrific gradation, afflicting all classes of society, from the king down to the wretched prisoner, but afflicting especially the priests, in order to show the impotence of the idols in whose name they spoke and acted. Here I must ask a question. What was the object of the Lord in performing so many miracles, that is, so many alterations of the laws of nature? Some say that the object of the Lord was the deliverance of the descendants of the Patriarchs from their secular chains, the deliverance of the people in whom all the families of the earth were to be blessed. As it is written, "And I have come down to deliver them out of the hand of Egypt, and to bring them out of that land,"[3] and this was doubtless a noble aim, for it proves the mercy of the Almighty towards all those who suffer, whether they be nations or individuals.

Others believe that the Lord's intention was to take revenge on those who had set His power at defiance and to inflict upon Pharaoh and his people so severe a punishment as to render them an ever-memorable warning unto all those who should follow in their footsteps. As it is written, "And I will stretch out my hand, and smite Egypt with all my wonders that I will do in the midst thereof."[4] This again proves the justice of the Lord,

---

[2] Exodus 5:2

[3] Exodus 3:8

[4] Exodus 3:20

who cannot suffer to see iniquity remain unpunished, and who, holding all men who do wrong, whatever their fortune and position, to be equally guilty, always bestows a punishment corresponding to the crime committed. The Lord, however, could have easily obtained these two objects without any great display of His. One moment, one word would have sufficed for the carrying out of His all-potent will. But the object of the Lord was even grander and more elevating, as the Scriptures clearly assert: "And ye shall know that I am the Lord your God, who bringeth you out from under the burden of the Egyptians."[5] During their two hundred and ten years of slavery, the Hebrews had almost forgotten the pure idea of the Divinity as bequeathed unto them by the Patriarchs; they had almost learned from their oppressors to worship that which is visible, manifest to our senses and material. And yet Israel, whom God had already called "my son, even my firstborn" was, as such, to exercise a decisive influence in the future over the whole human family; he was to become "the witness of the Lord" and the depositary of His law, of the eternal truths which are indispensable to the very existence of the world. He would therefore make Himself known to both nations, the faithful and the idolaters. He would perform before them such wonders as would oblige them to acknowledge Him as the true, the One God, the absolute Master of heaven and earth:

> All this I have done and more will I do, that ye, Israelites, my children, may recognise that I am the Lord.
>
> *Exodus 6:7*

[5] Exodus 6:7

> All this have I done, and more will I do, that Pharaoh and all heathens may know that none is like the Lord God.
>
> *Exodus 8:10*

And it is so the object which the Lord had in performing for Israel's glory and preservation, both in Egypt and in the wilderness, in Palestine and in the land of exile, so many great deeds which are engraved in the immortal pages of history, was that we should acknowledge Him as the Perfect Being to whom alone worship and adoration are due. And the object which He has still in achieving the marvels which we witness every day and every moment is to force us to know His greatness and immensity, compared with which we are much less than the worm which creeps upon the earth is, compared with us. Moses had failed in his first attempt to soften the heart of Pharaoh on behalf of the Hebrews. Severely rebuked by the tyrant, Moses saw the previously gloomy condition of his brethren become ever worse and intolerable. Then yielding to his impatience and to a feeling of despair, he addressed a complaint to the Lord. "Wherefore," he said, "hast Thou so evil entreated this people? Why is it that Thou hast sent me? for since I came to speak to Pharaoh in Thy name, he has done evil to this people, neither hast thou delivered this people at all."[6] Moses lacked faith for a moment, and in him, that was a great fault. The Lord, in His answer, made him aware of his condemnable shortcoming, for in a few words He mentioned His three cardinal attributes, which Moses ought never to have forgotten. "I am the Lord," He said unto Moses, "and I appeared unto Abraham, unto Isaac, and unto Jacob by the name of God Almighty, but by my name

6 Exodus 5:22-23

Adonai was I not known unto them."[7]

The three words: אלוהים *Elohim*, שדי *Shaddai*, ה' *Adonai*, imply the three great qualities which characterise the Lord, and by which He ought to be known and adored. They signify Justice, Omnipotence, Eternity.

By the word אלוהים Elohim, which is often applied in the Bible to human judges, God reminded Moses that He was the essence of Justice.

The Patriarchs had known Him by this attribute, for He had repeatedly commanded them "to do justice and judgment." Abraham saw that He was the upright "judge of all the earth," when He punished the four cities stained with the most abominable vices, and poured upon them His Divine fire, dooming them to utter destruction. In all their vicissitudes the Patriarchs could clearly see the effects of the Divine justice; and either the victory obtained by the 318 servants of Abraham against the four armies headed by Kedorlaomer, or the protection afforded to Isaac from the envious Philistines, or the final triumph of the unjustly tormented Joseph, were palpable proofs that the laws of justice cannot be trodden upon with impunity, and that the moral order established by the Creator between man and man cannot be broken without fatal results to the unscrupulous transgressors. Jeremiah explained this Divine quality in the right manner, when he said:

> For Thine eyes are open on the ways of the sons of men, to give everyone according to his ways, and according to the fruit of his doings.
>
> *Jeremiah 32:19*

[7] Exodus 6:2-3

His eye sees the torments of those who are unjustly oppressed, the blood unjustly spilt, the property unjustly usurped. With His ever-open ear He hears the complaint of the innocent, as He heard "the groaning of the children of Israel whom the Egyptians kept in bondage."[8] From whatever part of the earth the cry for help may come, from the palace or from the cottage, whether uttered by a widow or by an orphan, by a king or by a beggar, if it is really the complaint of innocence against iniquity, it will surely reach the ear of the Almighty, "Who," as our Sages teach, "is always ready to bestow a good reward upon those who walk before Him."[9]

But the Lord could not exercise the quality of Justice if He did not possess the attribute of Omnipotence.

If His power was limited, how could He dispense full punishment or full reward? But then the Lord is omnipotent; therefore, He called Himself El Shaddai, and "as such, He made Himself known unto the Patriarchs." In all the visions which He granted to them, in all the words which He addressed unto them, in all the circumstances in which He acted on their behalf, He always impressed them with the idea of His omnipotence. Oh, my dear brethren, God is great, God is immense; and who can doubt it? Is it necessary to reflect so profoundly in order to know that the Lord wields unlimited power? Look at His works. Raise your eyes and observe the majesty of the heavens, those stars which in their greatness move so regularly above our heads, and compared with which, the earth is but an imperceptible atom. What magnificence! Who is the artist who said: Let the sun be created and preside over the day; let the

8 Exodus 6:5

9 RaSH"I to Exodus 6:3

moon appear in the firmament and be the gentle queen of night? Who gave both existence and movement to that multitude of stars, which are as many suns, surrounded by their planets, followed by their satellites, on which they spread a softened reflection of their light? Who can be the author of so many marvels which our feeble mind can scarcely comprehend? And who but God can be the Creator, the Omnipotent Sovereign of the universe? "No one but God," said Isaiah, "bringeth out their host by number: He calleth them all by names, by the greatness of His might, for that He is strong in power: no one fails."[10]

God is invisible; yet we can see Him in His works, which on the one hand are governed by laws too regular to be ascribed to casualty; on the other, they are too far above mortal power to be attributed to man. A Roman Emperor was one day speaking with a Hebrew sage of the practices which constitute an almost impassable barrier between our nation and all other races, when he suddenly, exclaimed: "Since, as thou sayest, thy God is so powerful and the master of all created beings, I order thee to show Him unto me." An open disobedience to the order of a Roman Emperor would have been a sentence of death. Therefore, the sage answered: "Oh, my sovereign, I will do thy pleasure, if thou wilt only meet me tomorrow at noon, beyond the town in the open plain." When on the following day the emperor met the sage, he said, "Wilt thou point out to me at last this God of thine?"

"Raise thine eyes, O sire, and fix them upon that burning sun." The emperor was soon overpowered by the dazzling splendor of that great source of light. "Thou canst not," said the

[10] Isaiah 40:26

sage, "bear for one moment the light of the sun, which is one, and not even the greatest, of the manifold works of my God, and how wouldst thou gaze with thy mortal eyes at the omnipotent God Himself, of whom the angels, all human creatures, all animated beings constantly say: 'Holy, holy, holy is the Lord of hosts; the whole earth is full of His glory'?"[11]

And it is true: the universe is an open book which announces the omnipotence of its Author. Not to learn how to read therein is already highly condemnable in man, whom God made the ruler of the earth; but to disbelieve it and boldly to exhibit our skepticism by our actions, would be always a foolish and sometimes a dangerous undertaking. Canute the Second, king of England and Denmark, who lived some eight hundred years ago, was one of the most powerful and, what is better, one of the wisest kings. As it happens with princes and sovereigns, with the rich and the great, he was surrounded with courtiers who, foolish in their praises and exaggerated in their flattery, attributed to him those high qualities which belong only unto the Almighty. Unable to put a stop to their senseless adulation, he resolved to give them a severe but useful lesson. He assembled them one stormy day, on the seashore; the wind rose higher and higher, the billows appeared agitated by internal convulsions. "It is your opinion," said Canute to his courtiers, "that even the elements would obey my orders; I command the sea, therefore, to resume its calmness, and no longer to disturb our sports." But in that moment the gale became furious, and a wave as huge as a mountain fell upon the king and his courtiers and nearly swept them all into the sea. God, not man, "said the king to his terrified followers," God, not man, is omnipotent;

11 Isaiah 6:3

God let us praise, God let us adore, for "His kingdom rules over all."[12] The sea and its innumerable inhabitants, the mountains and their eternal snow, the cedar of Lebanon as well as the humblest flower, the regular phenomena which we see renewed every day, and the phenomena which, like the plagues of Egypt, seem to break the order of nature, and the cause of which we vainly attempt to discover, are so many trumpets by which God causes these words to sound in the ear of man: "Ye shall know that I am the Lord, the only one God, and that besides me, there is no Saviour."[13]

The point, however, on which the Lord laid more stress in His kind rebuke to Moses, was this third attribute, Eternity; without which both Justice and Omnipotence would become inefficient, useless.

That is the quality which is so beautifully expressed by the ineffable name, that Holy Name which we are forbidden to utter as it is written, and which, in token of our awe, veneration and even terror, we merely pronounce Adonai. In the Hebrew language alone there is one word which possesses the most comprehensive meaning, since it signifies eternity in its three parts: past, present, and future; it means that the Lord is not limited by time, since He Himself is time. We perishable creatures can look back to the time which has passed since our life began. We can look forward to the time which will elapse till our end comes; but our present consists merely of one atom, that in which we mention it. The Lord had no beginning, He will have no end; and His existence is, so to say, an everlasting present, because He does not change, and as He was, so He is

[12] Psalm 103:19

[13] Isaiah 43:11

and will be. "Thou art the same, and Thy years shall have no end."[14] When He said to Moses "I am the Lord," He meant that time is nothing unto Him, that His promise shall never fail, for the future is under His power, and His will is immutable. Reasons known to Him alone may delay His interference, but He will doubtlessly bestow His protection upon the weak against the strong, upon the innocent against the guilty, upon the oppressed against the oppressors, until justice is done:

> He is God; the faithful God, who keepeth covenant and mercy with them that love Him and keep His commandments to a thousand generations.
>
> *Deuteronomy 7:9*

So the object of the Lord's acts is that we should know Him in His essence and in His attributes. And surely, when we see ourselves surrounded by the marvels of God's creation, when we observe the order and harmony which prevail in the wonderful mechanism of the universe, we are forced to recognise that there is a God. But will that knowledge exercise no influence over us, over our mind and our character? How! When we are really and deeply convinced that the Lord is just and omnipotent, can we ever indulge in wicked actions, or even in wicked thoughts? At the idea of a judge whose will finds no obstacles, whose power is unlimited, a judge who is upright but inexorable, shall we not be deterred from walking in the path of vice, dishonesty, or crime? When we really understand what the eternity of God means, shall we, if tried by failure, or oppressed by misfortune, ever murmur against Him, exhibit impatience,

---

[14] Psalm 102:28

or want of faith? No; we shall hope in Him who rules time, who promises and is sure to keep His word, who knows the right moment to give assistance, to bring about the rescue of those that are unjustly oppressed, that suffer for the good cause, the cause of the Lord.

This knowledge of the Almighty is necessary to man, to whatever creed he may belong; it is as indispensable to his intellect as light is indispensable to his eyes; and just as a tender mother obliges her child to take the food which, from caprice, he sometimes rejects, so the Lord enforces His knowledge upon all the sons of men. When He has to deal with the good and the righteous, it is by His favors, by the deeds of His mercy, by bestowing upon them protection and untiring assistance, that He leads them to acquire the knowledge of His existence and omnipotence. He acted thus with Israel, to whom He said: "And ye shall know that I am the Lord your God, who bringeth you out from under the burden of the Egyptians."[15] But those that are naturally wicked, whose evil disposition prompts them to transgress even the laws of natural religion, are differently treated. It is by the means of hard blows, of terrific plagues, of heart - rending misfortunes, that the Lord enforces upon them the knowledge of His attributes, His justice, His omnipotence and His eternity, as it is written:

> For I will this time send all My plagues upon thine heart, and upon thy servants, and upon thy people, that thou mayest know that there is none like Me in all the earth.
>
> *Exodus 9:14*

[15] Exodus 6:7

Our sages said that "a precious jewel hung around the neck of Abraham."[16] It was not a talisman, an amulet, supposed by the superstitious to keep away the consequence of envy, of evil eye; the jewel was the knowledge of the Lord, of the one God, of the Omnipotent Being, that knowledge which Abraham disseminated among men; it was the spiritual jewel which ought to be treasured in the heart of every good man, of every true Israelite. We have inherited that jewel, we have it still. Oh, let us wear it with pride, for it is the noblest decoration. Let us preserve the knowledge of the Lord, let us teach it to our fellow creatures, and our mind will be elevated, our heart ennobled, our path enlightened, and our actions will bear the stamp of justice, we shall then be able to perform our mission, our destiny upon the earth in accordance with the words of Moses:

> Ye shall walk after the Lord your God and fear Him, and keep His commandments, and obey His voice, and ye shall serve Him, and cleave unto Him.
>
> *Deuteronomy 33:5*

✦

16 *Baba Batra* 16b

Zeman Ḥerutenu

Ḥakham Ben Zion Uziel[1]

Ḥakham Ben-Zion Meir Ḥai Uziel (1880-1953) was born in Jerusalem to an illustrious family. He was a leading *poseq* of his generation, a thinker, teacher, leader, and activist. He would serve the Jewish people in various capacities, culminating with his appointment as the first Sephardi Chief Rabbi of Israel in 1939.

Raised in Jerusalem, he studied with Sephardi and Ashkenazi sages alike, and thus became well steeped in the *halakhot* of both these worlds. These strong foundations were immensely formative and useful to him when he became a teacher in *Yeshibot*, and then in 1911 when he became *Ḥakham Bashi* (Chief Rabbi) of Jaffa.

He strove to raise the status of the Sephardi community there, and at the same time worked with his Ashkenazi counterpart, Chief Rabbi Abraham Yiṣḥaq Kook, to foster better inter-communal relations. During the First World War he fought for the protection of the Jews in the Land of Israel before being exiled to Damascus. After returning, he would serve as Chief

---

1 translation by Mord Maman

Rabbi of Salonika in Greece for two years, setting up schools and *Yeshibot*. Once back in Israel, he became Chief Rabbi of Tel Aviv before being elevated to the office of *Rishon LeṢiyon,* Chief Rabbi of Israel.

He authored many published volumes of responsa, such as *Mishpeṭei Uzi'el*, *Sha'arei Ụzi'el*, *Mikhmanei Ụzi'el* and *Hegyonei Ụzi'el*, with many unpublished writings still in manuscript form.

In both his literary output and his life, we see a Sage who was driven by a desire for unity — but also someone who understood the value of the Sephardi approach. When appointed Chief Rabbi of Jaffa, he spoke of his vision to heal the divisions between the Sephardi, Ashkenazi, and Yemenite communities. Ḥakham Uziel saw the historical events unfolding before his eyes in the Land of Israel and this imbued his life with a sense of urgency in demanding and furthering the unity of the Jewish people. He held that divisions were a product of the diaspora and that, as the Jewish people began to be in-gathered, it was time to shed these exilic constructs.

Yet this did not quell his Sephardi fervour. At the same time as working with his Ashkenazi and Yemenite colleagues he was working tirelessly to build Sephardi *Yeshibot* and train the next generation of Sephardi leaders.

The Sephardi approach to Talmud Torah, to philosophical enquiry, to science and general knowledge had to be preserved and transmitted to the next generation of Jews coming to build up the Land of Israel once more. He treasured that classical Sephardi approach, and whilst he was working to pass it on to fellow Sephardim, he also wished to share it with those in other Jewish traditions.

The following essay, "*Zeman Ḥerutenu,*" is from his *Mikhmanei Uziel*, 1, Gate 2, 7:1.

✦

The time of our freedom, the festival of Pesaḥ, possesses two aspects; namely, memory of emancipation and hope for the final redemption. On this holy night, when all Jews recline around their tables, reciting the *Haggada* with four cups of redemption, redemption is introduced with "next year in the land of Israel, free people," and concluded with "we thank You for our redemption and the restoration of our souls. Blessed are You, Lord, Who redeemed Israel."

This demonstrates that Freedom (*Ḥerut*) and Redemption (*Ge'ula*) are not synonymous concepts, but rather distinct ideas with distinct lessons. Freedom is the path to Redemption, and any Freedom not followed by Redemption is not complete, but fragmented, for it is to be doubted that it will be sustained!

This understanding clarifies the "four expressions of redemption" stated in regards to the Exodus from Egypt and which allude to the future and final redemption. It is for this redemption that Israel carried her soul during the Exodus and offered her soul, suffering with love all the endless and severe damages of exile. The four expressions are enumerated in the following paragraphs.

"I will free you from the labours of the Egyptians," and "and I will deliver you from their bondage."[1] *Their bondage* is not to be read as "מעבודתם", but rather "מעבדותם" *your bondage*, because removal from a state of slavery is not emancipation until the very slaves themselves are rid of the feelings of inferiority and servitude within themselves. In essence, this is achieved when individuals have been rescued from slavery and have achieved a sense of complete emancipation in which no situation nor

1 Exodus 6:6–7

further development will lead them back to that sorry state of slavery. Furthermore, they feel and know that they themselves have been enlisted to shatter the chains of slavery and to call out to those imprisoned in various predicaments. *This* is absolute liberty and total emancipation, where not a remnant of slavery survives. This liberty is the precursor to redemption, for a slave is not redeemed so long as he does not aspire to attain freedom and recognise himself a free person. Considering this we come to the final two expressions of freedom: "I will redeem you with an outstretched arm and through extraordinary chastisements," and "and I will take you to be My people, and I will be your God."[2]

The redemption from Egypt facilitated through an 'outstretched arm' and 'extraordinary chastisements' did not just redeem Israel from the slavery of Egypt and slavery in general; rather, it redeemed them from the impurity of Egypt and its gods, from the abominations of Egypt and its filth, and elevated them to the lofty recognition of God's providence over all the world, to bringing justice to the poor and needy and to saving oppressed from oppressors. The connection of Providence to the people of Israel makes them God's people and His legion, destined to fight with body and soul the war of truth, opposing falsehood and fabrication, rising to knowledge of the True God and clinging to His good and just ways for the success and happiness of mankind. This is *Torat Ha'adam*, the foundation of *Torat Yisra'el*, of which the entire aim is to elevate man from his lowliness and poverty, from his ignorance and impurity, to the lofty holiness of human life and the exalted and sublime moral level which guides one in all work and along paths – to walk in

2 Exodus 6:6-7

the good and just ways of God which give glory to those who do so and wonder to the entire human species, as the verse states:

> "and that He will set you, in fame and renown and glory, high above all the nations that He has made; and that you shall be, as He promised, a holy people to the Lord your God."
>
> *Deuteronomy 26:19*

The Essence of Freedom

Ḥerut is not merely the casting off of the yoke of slavery which has been forcibly placed upon oneself by others, for this is external and neglects to address one's essence. True *ḥerut* releases the slave from his lowliness and subjugation, not just to where freedom as power can be demonstrated, but, most importantly, to a state of freedom from those foreign ideologies which entered their mind through ignorance and a sorry state of being, in which they incorporated the dangerous, destructive idea: "How did those nations worship their gods? I too will follow those practises."[3]

This error did not come about because it was thought to be correct and fitting; rather, it came about through serving others. A slave may see their master act in such a way and believe that freedom would be mimicry and an imitation of their actions, as a monkey emulates a human. This is an incorrect freedom, not even fitting of the name, for the slavery of imitation is greater than the slavery of acquisition,[4] for even if one were physically acquired as is a Cana'anite slave, one still aspires to be free and attain that freedom through a monetary redemption or damage

3 Deuteronomy 12:30

4 *'Abdut Haḥiquy and 'Abdut Haqinyan*, respectively.

to tooth or eye or even by casting off the yoke of slavery by rebelling against one's master as a prisoner breaking out from jail. However, slavery of imitation is a lower, more disgraced form of slavery; one mired in this state cannot flee from it, and every passing day one settles deeper into slavery and servitude, which carries on to one's offspring for generations.

Thus do other nations enslave – once another nation is conquered, their gods and idols are added to the conquered nations' pantheon.

In Hebrew, the casting off of the yoke of slavery is termed "*ḥofesh*" (freedom), a state which can be reached by a Cana'anite slave, yet which will not ever be internalised, as the verse states, "he shall let him go free on account of his eye."[5] However, in *Leshon HaQodesh* the concept of *ḥerut* teaches of emancipation of soul and mind, their greatness which is not subjected to foreign influence. In this sense, the wisest of all men said: "Happy are you, O land whose king is a master (מלכך בן־חורים) and whose ministers dine at the proper time."[6]

What is a *melekh ben ḥorin*? He is one free from the control of any foreign power, who governs his kingdom of his own initiative in the spirit of the people's Torah and heritage of his fathers. Conversely, a *melekh na'ạr* is one lacking the independent ability or self–confidence to defend his beliefs, his land, and his people in body and spirit. He is tempted by any external brilliance, like a child distracted by anything that sparkles. Israel is a nation of *ben ḥorin* by nature, and by the merit of the heritage of their forefathers were brought out of Egypt,

---

5 Exodus 21:26. In the original essay, *shinav* (tooth) was mistakenly substituted for *'eino* (eye).

6 Ecclesiastes 10:17–18

from the house of bondage, to preserve their freedom even in the long and bitter exiles to come.

The Concept of Freedom

Our rabbis teach:

> "On account of four things Israel was redeemed from Egypt: they did not change their names, they did not change their language, they did not speak *lashon hara*, and not even one of them was found to be promiscuous.'"[7]

Language is more than a tool for the expression of one's desires and wishes to fulfil his needs, for it is also an expressive instrument for the conveyance of thoughts and ideas of the heart. The wisdom of language is to find suitable expressions for the wishes of the heart and mind. Based on this aspect of speech, our sages stated:

> "Due to the sin of vulgar speech, troubles abound, and harsh decrees are renewed, and the youth among the enemies of Israel, a euphemistic reference to Israel, die, and orphans and widows cry out for help and are not answered, as it is stated: 'Therefore the Lord shall have no joy in their young men, neither shall He have on their fatherless and widows; for everyone is ungodly and an evildoer, and every mouth speaks wantonness.'[8]...Anyone who speaks vulgarly, they deepen Gehenna for him."

Shabbat 33a

> "A person should always speak with clean language."

Pesaḥim 3a

---

7 *Vayiqra Rabbah* 32:5, *Midrash Tehillim* 114:4, *Bamidbar Rabbah* 2:22, *Shir Hashirim Rabbah* 4, *Mekhilta Bo* 5

8 Isaiah 9:16

The national tongue is not one which changes through the combination of letters, the swapping of pronunciations and the addition of phrases. The national tongue is that which expresses the morality of the nation; particularly, it does not merely express that which must be said but also the manner in which it shall be stated, the manner in which the lips express the heart's inclinations and reflect their level of morality. Therefore, Israel did not name its language "The Hebrew Language," instead giving it the unique name "The Holy Tongue," distinguishing it from all other languages which are mundane.

If you wish to understand the value of this language, learn it from that which the Holy Tongue utilises to teach the concept of freedom; namely *deror* (liberty): "You shall proclaim liberty throughout the land for all its inhabitants."[9]

This term imparts the Torah outlook, that man's freedom is natural. We are taught that the natural state of the nation is freedom, and it cannot be enslaved nor conform to servitude. Rather, it is a flying swallow (*deror*) that tweets and sings when free, but if taken captive refuses to eat to the point of death.[10]

The Names of Israel

The names of Israel do not solely distinguish between individuals, but identify one's essence or role in life, as we find with all the names of Israel found in the Torah and holy writings, beginning with Adam through later generations – they express the reason for one's being, and we observe that the addition of prefixes or suffixes connects them God's name.

---

9 Leviticus 25:10

10 See Ibn Ezra to Leviticus 25:10

There is a wondrous teaching of Ḥazal pertaining to this:

> "Rav Idi said, 'ה' at the beginning of the word and 'י' at the end comprise 'י-ה' which bears testimony for them that they are the sons of their fathers, and what is the reason? ' ששם עלו שבטים שבטי-יה עדות לישראל' – 'to which tribes would make pilgrimage, the tribes of the Lord'[11] that they are the sons of their fathers."[12]
>
> *Yalquṭ, Pinḥas*

The names of Israel indicate lineage and are to be considered names of honour. Each individual must take pride and find glory in their name and those of their ancestors, proclaiming, "I am a Jew and I fear the God of the world."[13] Language and

---

[11] Psalms 122:4

[12] Rashi to Numbers 26:5 s.v. משפחת החנכי THE FAMILY OF THE HANOCHITES: Because the heathen nations spoke slightingly of Israel, saying, "How can these trace their descent by their tribes? Do they think that the Egyptians did not overmaster their mothers? If they showed themselves master of their bodies, it is quite certain that they did so over those of their wives!". On this account the Holy One, blessed be He, set His name upon them: the letter ה on one side of their name and the letter י on the other side (חנכיה), to intimate: I bear testimony for them that they are the sons of their reputed fathers (and not of the Egyptians) (*Shir HaShirim Rabbah* 4:12). This it is that is expressed by David, (Psalms 122:4) שבטי יה עדות לישראל: "that the tribes bear the name of the Lord (יה) is a testimony regarding Israel" — this Divine Name (יה) bears testimony regarding their tribes (i.e. that they rightly attach themselves to those tribes to which they claim to belong). On this account in the case of all of them it is written החנכי and הפלואי but in the case of ימנה (v. 44) it was not felt necessary to state "of the family of הימני", because the Divine Name is already attached to it — the י at the beginning and the ה at the end (ימנה) (*Yalqut Shimoni* on Torah 773).

[13] Jonah 1:9

names are significant indicators and offer faithful testimony regarding the spiritual emancipation of the nation, for no change of circumstance nor of values has annulled its honour nor its freedom; thus no force can destroy it, yet the question that remains for us and for everyone is: from where do these forces draw their vitality, expressed as the Holy Tongue and Jewish names?

The 'Mysteries' of the Nation and the Sanctity of the Family

In answering this question our Rabbis stated that the people must not reveal their mysteries nor engage in forbidden sexual relationships.

The "mysteries" of the nation are the latent reserves of faith hidden in the individual soul and national collective soul. These must not be revealed, for there exists no concrete method to express their depth and profundity; these mysteries are the life force sustaining eternal life, charging it with strength and power. These mysteries are only to be found in children of the nation pure and holy from the time of their formation, not in those conceived from forbidden relationships, for these produce rude and untrustworthy children. Trustworthy children, formed in holiness and born in sanctity, whose bodies bear the eternal covenant of Judaism, are capable of guarding the language of the nation and the names of the heritage of the forefathers in sanctity and purity, for these are the signs and testimony of their freedom.

Slavery and Liberty

The Torah elevates the entire nation to the heightened perspective that each Jew is essentially and intrinsically free, and that all Israel are descendants of kings, as stated in the Talmud: "All of Israel are princes"[14]; "all of Israel are fit for royalty."[15]

Man, created in God's image, with God's providence guiding his paths and deeds, cannot become the physical property of another, not by strength nor by punitive force as was the custom of earlier peoples – the first born of a slave girl found behind the millstone – and as observed today with punitive measures of backbreaking labour or internment in jail. Furthermore, one does not retain the agency to sell oneself into slavery, even for several years: "For it is to Me that the Israelites are servants"[16]; "For they are My servants, whom I freed from the land of Egypt; they may not give themselves over into servitude."[17]

The Torah only permitted one to sell oneself for sustenance when there exists no other alternative, as stated clearly in the halakhic literature:

> "He is not permitted to sell himself and put the money away or buy merchandise or utensils with it, or give it to a creditor. He can sell his freedom only if he needs the money for food."
>
> *RaMBa"M, MT Ạbadim 1:1*

When, in necessary circumstances, this occurs, it is only permitted until the Jubilee Year, as RaMBa"M states – that upon the start of Jubilee Year the slave is completely emancipated, even if sold to a gentile. Indeed, there do exist instances in which a Jew may be sold against their will by a *Bet Din*, under

14 *Shabbat* 67a, *Baba Meṣia* 113b

15 *Horayot* 13a

16 Leviticus 25:55

17 Leviticus 25:42

are two stipulations. First, this person may only be sold as a result of theft which they were unable to repay, as the verse states, "if he lacks the means, he shall be sold for his theft."[18] RaMBa"M writes: "With the exception of a thief, the court may not sell any Israelite."[19]

This is not a punitive measure, rather a provision for a pauper to find rectification in the event that they are unable to pay back their theft. Second, sale by the *Bet Din* retains a further stipulation: "it sells him only to an Israelite or to a true proselyte,"[20] and: "it only sells this person for six years, or earlier in the event of a *Yobel*."[21]

In any event, a Hebrew slave (*'Ebed 'Ivri*) is not sold at the public auction stand as slaves are commonly sold, for the verse states, "they must not be sold as slaves are sold."[22] Instead, "he should rather be sold privately and politely."[23]

In light of this, the purchaser of a Hebrew slave is prohibited from working him in the absence of a defined time allowance, nor may he assign him degrading work, nor work without purpose, nor public work unless it was his job beforehand.[24] Furthermore, the master must treat the Hebrew slave as an equal in terms of food, drink, clothing and living quarters, as we find written: "Whoever purchases a Hebrew servant purchases a master for himself."[25]

18 Exodus 22:2
19 *Hilkhot Ạbadim* 1:1
20 *Ibid.* 1:3
21 *Ibid.* 2:2
22 Leviticus 25:42
23 *Hilkhot Ạbadim* 1:5
24 *Ibid.* 1:6–7
25 *Ibid.* 1:9

The sum of the matter is that a Hebrew slave is to be considered hired help for dignified work for a number of years, and that his sale by the *Bet Din* is not done in a degrading manner, and that he is freed after a number of years or upon the arrival of the Jubilee Year – even against his will, as no person from Israel rules over oneself to the extent that one can make oneself a permanent slave or debase oneself in lowering one's value.

The Torah is imposes harsh strictures regarding the punishment awaiting one who wishes to retain slaves indefinitely, as the prophet says:

> "Thus said the Lord: You would not obey Me and proclaim a release, each to his kinsman and countryman. Lo! I proclaim your release—declares the Lord—to the sword, to pestilence…"
>
> *Jeremiah 34:17*

However, there exist those who mock the Torah in that it permits the physical purchase of a Cana'anite slave, but they must not mock, rather understand, that this purchase is permitted solely when this individual had been sold to his brethren under certain circumstances; even so, domination of his body is prohibited, for if this person were injured in one of the tips of their limbs or even their eye or tooth they go free[26], and "if a master killed their slave they would be put to death for this, for the Torah only permitted striking a slave with a rod, stick or strap but not a murderous blow."[27]

The Torah does permit giving the Cana'anite slave backbreaking labour, though it would be an act of piety and the

---

26 *Ibid.* 5:4

27 *Hilkhot Roṣe'aḥ ve'Shemirat Hanefesh* 2:14

way of the wise to have mercy and pursue justice and not intensify the yoke over one's slave, rather feed them and satiate them with all manner of food and drink, not to shout at them excessively nor show them anger, rather to speak gently to them gently and listen to their concerns, as apparent from the words of Job: "Did I ever brush aside the case of my servants, man or maid when they made a complaint against me?... Did not He who made me in my mother's belly make him? Did not One form us both in the womb?"[28]

One should act towards them with Godly traits:

> In speaking of the divine attributes, which he has commanded us to imitate, the psalmist says: "His mercy is over all his works."[29] Whoever is merciful will receive mercy, as it is written: "He will be merciful and compassionate to you and multiply you"[30]
>
> *Hilkhot Ạbadim 9:8*

From here it is observed that the permission granted by the Torah to acquire a Cana'anite slave is for his own benefit, to save him from their Cana'anite brethren by preventing his cruel enslavement at their hands, where he would be subjugated until his death. This understanding adds comprehension to the following laws:

> "When a person sells his slave to a gentile, the slave is released as a free man. We compel the previous owner to buy him back from the gentiles at even ten times his value. He then composes a bill of release for him, and the slave is released."

28 Job 31:13, 15
29 Psalms 145:9
30 Deuteronomy 13:18

> "If a person sells his slave to one of the servants of a king or his officers, despite the fact that the seller fears them, the slave receives his freedom. For he could have appeased them with other money."
>
> *Hilkhot Ạbadim 8:13*

Thus it is clarified that the permission to enslave even a Cana'anite is accompanied by myriad rules and regulations for his benefit, for alternatively he would have fallen into permanent slavery amongst his brethren. Thus he is saved from such disgrace and loss of independence and can be purchased by a Jew, under whose mastership he will be treated with kindness and mercy.

From this perspective we may evaluate the actions of the nations towards us who we have encountered in our bitter exile. Is it possible to quantify the innocent blood they spilt like water, the robbery of the poor and the groaning of the destitute, victimised for no reason? Consider the decrees of forced conversion and apostasy, the harsh insults with no end nor limit leading Israel to complain bitterly:

> "Is Israel a bondman? Is he a home-born slave? Then why is he given over to plunder? Lions have roared over him, have raised their cries. They have made his land a waste, His cities desolate, without inhabitants."
>
> *Jeremiah 2:14-15*

Yet still, Israel does not betray its innate freedom. She firmly grasps her belief that she is called by the creator of the world, "to bind up the wounded of heart, To proclaim release to the captives, Liberation to the imprisoned; To proclaim a year of the Lord's favour and a day of vindication by our God."[31]

Freedom of the Mind

Israel's emancipation is not restricted to freedom of body and soul, for there also exists a higher form of emancipation – freedom of mind and thought from all hallucination and superstition, fatal and false beliefs, omens, magic and enquiry of the dead, and inconsistencies which are enough to drive one insane. This lofty freedom, which instils free will in all one's deeds and actions, elevating one above an existence predicated upon mere luck, as we are commanded "be wholehearted with the Lord your God,"[32] and "and do not be dismayed by portents in the sky."[33] From this our sages learnt, "there exists no *mazal* for Israel."[34]

This freedom, the heritage of the assembly of Jacob, was fortified at the revelation at Sinai, where the Torah of freedom was received, the Torah which saved our ancestors and us from servitude to the nations and from the Angel of Death himself, as our sages have stated: "'Engraved (*ḥarut*) on the Tablets' – do not read '*ḥarut*' (engraved), rather '*ḥerut*' (freedom) from subjugation to nations, and freedom from the Angel of Death. As stated by the Lord, He shall rule over all nations save this one, which was given freedom."[35]

31 Isaiah 61:1

32 Deuteronomy 18:13

33 Jeremiah 10:2

34 *Shabbat* 156b

35 *Shemot Rabbah* 41

The Servitude of Freedom

Personal and national freedom is accompanied by a responsibility which leads to a servitude of sorts, a pleasant one at that. Those who claim complete freedom propose, "'I shall be safe, though I follow my own wilful heart'—to the utter ruin of moist and dry alike."[36] Alternatively, they will act in whatever manner they see fit, as there is no ultimate accountability for their actions. An unrestrained freedom, however, is damaging and destructive, demoting its subjects to the level of a talking beast.

Considering this, freedom of choice bestows grave responsibility and demands meticulousness in all deeds, holding one accountable to oneself, one's people, the Torah of Life and the Creator of man. This responsibility obligates one to turn from evil and choose good. Unshackled freedom lowers one from cultured heights, condemning him to eternal slavery in the servitude of unceasing pleasure-seeking. Conversely, recognition of the reality of judgement, the actuality of reward and punishment and ethics of Torah as they manifest in the life of a person and in the family, is true freedom.

Those lacking understanding believe that a fundamental aspect of freedom is casting off the yoke of Heaven in addition to those of national and communal significance; in the name of freedom do these individuals claim that achieving freedom is to be free from royal taxes or national responsibilities. These claims are made in the name of freedom, yet the claimants are slaves, wounded by blind selfishness and utmost savagery. All freedom which is not partnered with Torah is one of dereliction and

---

[36] Deuteronomy 29:18

anarchy, which brings chaos to the world. Freedom of the individual and the nation is defined by observance of the Torah of ethics; it is delimited by friendship, true faith, and philosophy. He who proudly violates these considerations is a tortuous being, a wild animal. Man, by nature, is a social being, and it is impossible for such a being to thrive without a form of leadership which regulates his actions, as RaMBa"M proposes: "I therefore maintain that the Law, though not a product of Nature, is nevertheless not entirely foreign to Nature."[37]

Indeed, because of man's social nature, a fundamental condition to his existence and progress, God created the human makeup to necessitate the need for leadership, which manifests in the roles of prophets and judges, and kings and provincial rulers: "Should a man act presumptuously and disregard the priest charged with serving there the Lord your God, or the magistrate, that man shall die"[38]; "you shall be free to set a king over yourself."[39] For his fear shall be over you; the Torah is unique in that state rulers are sanctified with the holiness of the Torah, thus intertwining terrestrial and Heavenly kingdoms.

Those who believe that freedom is achieved solely through abandonment of the community are mistaken, for freedom is a battle, but a freedom of separation shall precipitate death. To illustrate this mistaken approach, we turn to the commandments pertaining to Passover, which are characterised by two remembrances, one in the form of restraint – refraining from consuming *ḥameṣ*, the other in offering the Pascal lamb. Regarding both the verse states, "[and one who] refrains from

---

37 *Guide for the Perplexed* 2:40

38 Deuteronomy 17:12

39 Deuteronomy 17:15

offering the Passover sacrifice, that person shall be cut off from his kin"[40]; "for whoever eats leavened bread from the first day to the seventh day, that person shall be cut off."[41]

Individual freedom is part and parcel of national freedom. The individual is obligated to sanctify the holiness of the people, guarding national obligations both passively and actively. An arbitrary approach is not an indicator of freedom or greatness, rather it indicates intellectual and spiritual surrender to that appears to be free.

Freedom and Redemption

Freedom which removes bitterness, calls for liberty, eliminates the barriers of oppression and the ropes of exile, is the foyer to the palace of redemption. This redemption is a noble quality, by which one obtains purity of soul and heart, able to be bestowed upon others, and much like much human endeavour this may manifest in diverse ways. Take, for example, craftwork, in which an object might be glued to a material, yet does not integrate and merge with it; there exist other act which pierce deep, uniting and bringing two elements together in the aspect of "come near to me and redeem me"[42]; "and I will put My spirit into you."[43]

This redemption, which shapes and defines an individual and the nation as a whole, can only be attained through great effort and immense sacrifice, as the verse states, "I will redeem you with an outstretched arm and through extraordinary

40 Numbers 9:13

41 Exodus 12:15

42 Psalms 69:19

43 Ezekiel 36:27

chastisements."[44] Each individual and the nation as a whole strives to achieve redemption and build upon it, and achieve its goals; to live a fulfilling life filled with culture and Torah, to create a redeeming national autonomy which serves as a source of salvation and blessing for generations after them and for all mankind. This redemption is initially embedded in the knowledge of God, which exists to uplift the individual to the highest summit; it gives that individual pleasance in life and eternal spirit for the generations to come, and it is for this redemption that every soul thirsts: "I long, I yearn for the courts of the Lord."[45]

However, along the paths of providence there are two routes: The path of intellect understanding, the path of study with Divine assistance in the form of prophecy, or the path of Divine revelation in His wondrous actions, which illuminate the eyes and the darkness of the heart, illuminating the paths of our lives before it. The first way is achieved on an individual basis; achieving this will lead only to a personal intellectual knowledge which cannot be spoken of as it cannot be expressed, and when it is, it may only be done so soothingly. Know that even the master of all prophets, who spoke face to face and achieved the most wondrous life achievements was nevertheless required to beg, "oh, let me behold Your Presence!"[46] Yet even he was told "man may not see Me and live."[47]

Even the spiritual forms which carry the Heavenly Throne, as it were, cannot point and say, "this is my God" and "where is

---

44 Exodus 6:6
45 Psalms 84:3
46 Exodus 33:18
47 Exodus 33:20

the place of His glory?" However, God's revelation in His wonders is the revelation of the Divine Presence, which may be perceived through His traits and paths; "this is My God, and I shall enshrine him"[48] as they had faith in the Lord and His servant Moses. Faith is fixed within the spirit.

Yet this is still not complete, for it only opens the windows to the light; it is the sound of the *Shofar* that awakens one from slumber. Only when one combines this call with the reality the nation, uniting aspects of body and soul, shall the final and full redemption come.

> "See, a time is coming—declares the Lord—when I will make a new covenant with the House of Israel and the House of Judah. It will not be like the covenant I made with their fathers...But such is the covenant I will make with the House of Israel after these days—declares the Lord: I will put My Teaching into their inmost being and inscribe it upon their hearts. Then I will be their God, and they shall be My people."
>
> *Jeremiah 31: 31-33*

> "And I will take you to be My people, and I will be your God."
>
> *Exodus 6:7*

✦

[48] Exodus 15:2

Insights from the Present

By Selected Teachers & Contributors of The Ḥabura

In *Nisan*, They will be Redeemed

Rabbi Ratzon Arusi[1]

Rabbi Dr. Ratzon Arusi is Chief Rabbi of Kiryat Ono, a member of Israel's Chief Rabbinate Council, and founder of Halikhot Am Yisra'el Institute. Rabbi Arusi has a Ph.D. in law from Tel Aviv University, and lectures on Jewish law at Bar-Ilan University. He heads Kiryat Ono's rabbinical court for monetary law. A student of Rabbi Yosef Qafih *a"h*, Rabbi Arusi is a respected leader in the Yemenite and Sephardi community, and in the Jewish world at large.

[1] translation by Avner Yeshurun and Eli Shaubi

Well-known are the words of our sages of blessed memory: "In *Nisan* they were redeemed; *in Nisan they will be redeemed*."[1] But these words only represent R. Joshua's opinion. It seems that few are familiar with R. Eliẹzer's opinion (even though they are both cited in the same source): "In *Nisan* they were redeemed; *in Tishri they will be redeemed*." It is possible that since they both agree that "In *Nisan* they were redeemed," the view that they will be redeemed in *Nisan* became more widely known. It is worth clarifying – what is the nature of this future redemption? When shall it occur – not only in terms of months, but also in terms of years?

The Dispute Between R. Eliẹzer and R. Joshua

It ought to be noted that R. Eliẹzer and R. Joshua disagreed not only regarding the time of the future redemption, but also on the time of creation, and on various times related to the nation's Patriarchs and Matriarchs. According to R. Eliẹzer:

> In *Tishri*, the world was created. In *Tishri*, the Patriarchs were born. In *Tishri*, the Patriarchs passed. On Passover, Isaac was born. On *Rosh Hashana*, Sarah, Rachel, and Hannah were remembered. On *Rosh Hashana*, Joseph came out of prison. On *Rosh Hashana*, our forefathers' enslavement in Egypt ceased. In *Nisan*, they were redeemed; in *Tishri*, they will be redeemed.
>
> *Rosh Hashana* 11a

1 *Rosh Hashana* 11a

In contrast to R. Eliẹzer, R. Joshua states:

> In *Nisan*, the world was created. In *Nisan*, the Patriarchs were born. In *Nisan*, the Patriarchs passed. On Passover, Isaac was born. On *Rosh Hashana*, Sarah, Rachel, and Hannah were remembered. On *Rosh Hashana*, Joseph came out of prison. On *Rosh Hashana*, our forefathers' enslavement in Egypt ceased. In *Nisan*, they were redeemed; in *Nisan*, they will be redeemed.
>
> *Ibid.*

Matters of Agreement Between R. Eliẹzer and R. Joshua

We see, then, that the past redemption from Egypt is not a subject of dispute, as both R. Eliẹzer and R. Joshua concur that our forefathers' enslavement in Egypt ceased on *Rosh Hashana*, and that they were redeemed in *Nisan*. Likewise, they concur that Isaac was born on Passover. They also agree that the Matriarchs Sarah, Rachel, and Hannah were remembered on Rosh Hashana by being given perpetual seen; and that Joseph was remembered on Rosh Hashana, in that he came out of prison. In this respect, it is possible that the cessation of our forefathers' enslavement on *Rosh Hashana* is also a remembrance. For according to all, *Rosh Hashana* is the Day of Remembrance.

The dispute between them is: According to R. Eliẹzer, the world was created in *Tishri*; the future redemption will be in *Tishri*; and the Patriarchs were born and passed in *Tishri*. According to R. Joshua, the world was created in *Nisan*; the future redemption will be in *Nisan*; and the Patriarchs were born and passed in *Nisan*.

We may summarise as follows the points of consensus between R. Eliẹzer and R. Joshua:

- The time of creation and that of the future redemption correspond to one another.
- The time of creation and that of the future redemption correspond to the time of the Patriarchs' births and the time of their deaths.
- The time of the Exodus from Egypt and that of Isaac's birth correspond to one another.
- The Matriarchs' remembrance and the time of Joseph's remembrance correspond to the time of our forefathers' remembrance in Egypt, and that of the remembrance of all worldly creatures each year.

We may therefore posit that in Judaism, the universal and the cosmological are always tied to the national. So it is in the case of creation and the future redemption; so it is in the case of the births and deaths of the Patriarchs of our nation; and so it is in the case of the remembrance of all worldly creatures and the remembrance of our nation in Egypt. Likewise, the Exodus from Egypt corresponds to our patriarch Isaac's birth, who, for some reason, was singled out from among all the other Patriarchs with regard to the time of his birth.

The Castle has a Master, and the Nation has a Father

Consider the facts that both R. Eliẹzer and R. Joshua agree that the time of creation corresponds to the time of the future redemption, just that R. Eliẹzer places them in *Tishri* whereas R. Joshua places them in *Nisan*; and that both of them agree that the time of the births of the nation's Patriarchs correspond to the time of their deaths, just that R. Eliẹzer places them in *Tishri* whereas R. Joshua places them in *Nisan*; and that both of them agree that *Rosh Hashana* is the Day of Accounting, the Day of Judgement and Remembrance, for all worldly creatures, especially for Israel, and that the Matriarchs were remembered on *Rosh Hashana*, and that Joseph was remembered for freedom on *Rosh Hashana*, and that our forefathers in Egypt were remembered [for deliverance] from bondage to freedom on *Rosh Hashana* – all these facts teach us that both R. Eliẹzer and R. Joshua agree on the religious principles of Judaism.

For both agree that the created world is neither accidental nor a natural occurrence, and that the nation of Israel's existence is not an accidental national occurrence. Rather, there is a Master to the castle: God. There is a Father of the nation: God.

The world was created by God, after an absolute void, and the created world continues to exist at every moment and every second because of God's very existence and according to His will. And God's will is that man, who was created in His image, shall be purposeful and ethical in his behaviour and in his way of life; and that man shall be judged for life or death according to his deeds, and that humanity at large shall be judged for perpetuation or annihilation according to its deeds, and so too shall the world be judged for perpetuation or destruction.

Our nation was founded by God through Abraham, at *Berit ben HaBetarim*, that his offspring through Isaac, who were enslaved in Egypt, shall be God's nation, an ethical nation that has a purpose, and that it shall be a kingdom of priests and a holy nation for all humanity and a light unto the nations.

The Temple and the Sanctification of the Name

Indeed, the number of years of Israel's exile in Egypt, according to *Berit ben HaBetarim* begins with Isaac's birth. This might be the reason that both Isaac's birth and the Exodus from Egypt are placed in *Nisan*, according to all opinions.

Still, however, we must recognise that Isaac himself never went down to Egypt, but rather Jacob did, and that Isaac had another son, Esau. It seems therefore more fitting that Jacob be singled out, not Isaac. Nevertheless, there are some respects in which Isaac surpasses the other Patriarchs, for he sacrificed himself for God's will, to be bound as a perfect burnt-offering. This is the foundation for sanctifying God's name. Moreover, by this deed he sanctified the place upon which he was bound, to be an eternal House of Sanctity (*Bet Miqdash*), from which Judaism will draw sanctity for itself and for all humanity.

Likewise, our Patriarch Isaac never left the Holy Land; he was born in it, lived in it, and died in it. For this reason, his birth is attributed to Nisan, since it is the foundation for the birth of the nation with the Exodus of Egypt, as God's nation, in Nisan.

Being and Purpose

The Talmud there[2] states that R. Eliẹzer, who states that the world was created in *Tishri*, based his opinion on the fact that God stated among the accounts of creation, "Let the Earth sprout forth vegetation, herbs yielding seed,"[3] and *Tishri* is the month during which the land sprouts vegetation and fruit-

2 *Ibid.*

3 Genesis 1:11

bearing trees, and during which rain falls upon the earth, causing plants to grow.

R. Joshua, on the other hand, who states that the world was created in *Nisan*, based his opinion on the fact that it is stated among the accounts of creation, "The Earth produced vegetation, herbs yielding seed after its kind, and trees bearing fruit,"[4] and *Nisan* is the month during which the land is filled with vegetation and the trees produce fruit, and beast and fowl mate.

R. Eliẹzer ultimately places the emphasis on the beginning of existence, whereas R. Joshua places the emphasis on existence once it is already in existence, as well as on the purposefulness present in existence. It is therefore possible that R. Eliẹzer subscribes to the view that this created world has a beginning and an end, and that the End of Days will be accompanied by cosmological events, due to the physical world's fulfillment of its very existence. This is similar to the way in which the Patriarchs' lives in this world have completeness: God fills their days, and when they fulfill themselves to the fullest in this world, they die, i.e. they are removed from among us and move on to another world, the world of truth and eternity.

In contrast, it is possible that R. Joshua subscribes to the view that the sole difference between this world and the Days of the Messiah is subservience to [foreign] kingdoms.[5] For the primary point regarding creation in general, and the Patriarchs in particular, is each one's purpose, not the beginning of their existence or their existence itself. Though our forefathers were

4 *Ibid.*, v.12

5 This is the opinion of Samuel in *Shabbat* 151b; RaMBa"M decided according to him (*Hilkhot Melakhim* 12:1-2).

freed from slavery on *Rosh Hashana*, they only left Egypt and became servants of God in *Nisan*. Likewise, our nation in particular, and humanity in general, shall attain their purpose at the End of Days, insofar as all will be unified around faith in God. For even though slavery ceased from upon our forefathers already from *Tishri*, thus rendering them servants of Pharaoh no longer, they had yet to become servants of God. They became God's servants only in *Nisan*, when they were commanded by God in the Paschal lamb and circumcision, and performed them accordingly.

The Future Redemption – Cataclysmic National and International Occurrences

The future redemption, as described by the prophets, will entail gentile wars in Jerusalem, the wars of Gog and Magog, and the building of the Temple on the holy mountain in Jerusalem by the Messiah King.

> It shall come to pass, at the End of Days, the mount of the Lord's house shall stand firm above the mountains, and tower above the hills, and all the nations shall stream to it. Many peoples shall go, saying, "Come, let us go up to the mount of the Lord, to the house of the God of Jacob, that He may instruct us in His ways, and that we may walk in His paths." For from Zion shall instruction come forth, and the word of the Lord from Jerusalem.
>
> *Isaiah 2:2-3*[6]

The period referred to is the Messianic era and the time of the ingathering of the exiles.[7] It is the period of the wars of Gog and

6 Cf. Micah 4:1-3

7 R. David Qimḥi, commentary to Micah 4:11

Magog.[8] In those days, each nation shall return to its homeland, and all shall be "under the sovereignty of Israel."[9]

Cataclysmic national and international events such as these are processes that take place over many years. They do not occur in a number of days, nor in one month. Thus, the "time" of the future redemption, established by R. Eliẹzer as *Tishri*, and R. Joshua as *Nisan*, begs exposition.

The Dedication of the Third Temple in *Nisan*

As is known, Ezekiel prophesied the building of a Third Temple, which, according to our sages of blessed memory, will stand eternally. He further prophesied that the completion-offerings will be offered at the Third Temple's dedication, and that the time of that offering will be "on the first (i.e. the first month, namely *Nisan*), on the first of the month."[10] R. David Qimḥi writes:

> "On the first" – this refers to the month of *Nisan*, which is *the month of redemption, during which Israel was redeemed from Egypt, and during which they will be redeemed in the future.* On the first of the month, they shall dedicate the altar with offerings...This verse is a proof for R. Joshua, *that in the future they will be redeemed in Nisan.* For if the redemption were to occur in *Tishri*, how is it possible that they would refrain from giving offerings on the altar, from cleansing upon it, and from atoning the Temple until the following *Nisan*? What he meant by saying that in the future they will be redeemed in *Nisan* is not that they will leave their exile in *Nisan*; rather, *they will leave [their exile] and go up [to Israel] before Nisan, such that by the first of Nisan the building of the Temple shall be completed, and they*

---

8 *Meṣudat David* to *ibid.*

9 R. David Qimḥi, commentary to Jeremiah 48:47

10 Ezekiel 45:18

> *will dedicate the altar on the first of Nisan.* This is also what was done with regards to the *Mishkan*: On the first of *Nisan*, Aaron began the service at the altar, just that that was preceded by the seven days of completion, during which Moses performed the service…"
>
> *Commentary to Ezekiel 45:18*

From R. Qimḥi's words we learn that when our sages of blessed memory state that on a certain month they were – or will be – redeemed, they do not refer to the entire redemptive process and to all the integral, great events that comprise the redemption. For in order to build the Temple, it is necessary that Israel return to its land and have sovereignty over it. Events such as these do not occur in a matter of days, nor in one month. It is the peak of these occurrences that is fit for designation as the time of redemption; for instance, the dedication of the Third Temple, which will take place on the first of *Nisan*, caused our sages of blessed memory to establish, and rightfully so, that in the future we will be redeemed in *Nisan*.

Repentance is a Prerequisite for the Future Redemption

From R. David Qimḥi's words, we have learnt that Ezekiel's words about the time of the dedication of the Third Temple support R. Joshua, who states that in the future we will be redeemed in *Nisan*. But there is a difficulty with R. Qimḥi's words: Certainly, R. Eliẹzer also saw these words of Ezekiel! Would R. Eliẹzer dispute that the Third Temple will be dedicated on the first of *Nisan*?

We ought to assume that R. Eliẹzer admits that the dedication of the Third Temple will be on the first of *Nisan*. If so, why does he not identify the future redemption with the greatest climax of all its events, the building of the Third Temple and its dedication?!

We have already seen that R. Eliẹzer and R. Joshua differ in their approach and attitude towards major cataclysmic events – whether the beginning of their coming into being should be the starting point from which to consider them, as in the view of R. Eliẹzer, or whether their purpose, once they have already come into being, having ripened and borne fruit, as is the view of R. Joshua.

We have further found that R. Eliẹzer is of the view that *"if Israel repents, they are redeemed."*[11] It is possible that it is because of this opinion of his, that he said that they will be redeemed in *Tishri*, i.e. during the days of judgement and repentance that will precede the events of redemption. The reason they will be during those days, days of our nation's repentance, is precisely because only repentance can pave the way for redemptive events to occur.

It ought to be noted that R. Joshua agrees with R. Eliẹzer that repentance is a prerequisite for redemption. He only disagreed with him that the prerequisite for redemption is repentance specifically during the days of judgement and repentance. This is evident from his response to R. Eliẹzer:

> "[Can one say that] if they do not repent, they are not redeemed?! Rather, the Holy One (blessed is He), would appoint a king over them whose decrees are as harsh as Haman's, and Israel would repent and return to the right path."
>
> *Sanhedrin 97b*

11 *Sanhedrin* 97b

That is, according to R. Joshua, even if the nation does not repent on its own, the reality of redemption is not to be discarded. For it is possible that God will bring about the events that precede redemption and that simultaneously the nation will repent, as was the case with the appearance of Haman, which caused the nation to repent and subsequently be redeemed.

If you look closely at this dispute between R. Joshua and R. Eliẹzer,[12] you will realise that the crux of what R. Joshua intended is that God will assist the nation to repent when He redeems them. In light of this, then, R. Eliẹzer is seemingly of the view that only when the nation repents organically, during the days of judgement and repentance, that shall they be worthy of redemption. In contrast, R. Joshua is of the view that even if the nation does not repent on their own, God will assist them to repent, even by force, so that He may redeem them.

"As in the days of your exodus from Egypt, I shall show him wonders"

Indeed, the prophet Micah prophesied, "As in the days of your exodus from Egypt, I shall show him wonders."[13] That is, just as miracles and wonders were integrated into the Exodus from Egypt, so in the future, when He will redeem our nation, He shall induce miracles and wonders.

R. David Qimḥi[14] writes that these miracles and wonders are related to the wars of Gog and Magog in the holy city of Jerusalem. There is no doubt that the miracle of the

[12] *Ibid.*, 97b-98a
[13] Micah 7:15
[14] Commentary to Micah 7:16

Resurrection of the Dead is one of those miracles that will be performed at that time, prior to the era of the Messiah or following it.[15] Just as the miracles during the Exodus from Egypt were intended to instill faith in God and in His providence, into the hearts of our forefathers and into the hearts of the nations of the world, so too the miracles and wonders that will occur, and with even greater intensity, at the End of Days. For they are intended to bring about our nation's repentance, as well as the repentance of the nations of the world, so that all will be united around faith in God; and that Israel return to be a kingdom of priests and a holy nation, and a light unto the nations.

The building of a Third Temple shall guarantee the actualisation of this unique characteristic of Israel, as well as the actualisation of their destiny. And so, when the nations of the world will be influenced by Israel, in the era of the Third Temple, they shall say:

> "'Come, let us go up to the mount of the Lord, to the house of the God of Jacob, that He may instruct us in His ways, and that we may walk in His paths.' For from Zion shall instruction come forth, and the word of the Lord from Jerusalem."
>
> *Micah 4:2*

Since the Third Temple is to be the greatest climax of Israel's redemption and of all of humanity, it will be dedicated, as we have stated according to all opinions, in *Nisan*; for this reason, R. Joshua's view – that they will be redeemed in *Nisan* – became widespread. For even if our nation will not repent on its own, God shall return us to Him, even if by means of His miracles

15 RaMBa"M, *Treatise on the Resurrection of the Dead*

and wonders. Nonetheless, when we do repent and are redeemed, the Third Temple shall be built, for eternity, and shall be dedicated in *Nisan*; then will we be able to fulfil our destiny to be a kingdom of priests and a holy nation, and a light unto all humanity. In that *Nisan*, we shall be eternally redeemed.

✦

On Time and Freedom

Senior Rabbi Joseph Dweck

Rabbi Joseph Dweck is the Senior Rabbi of the S&P Sephardi Community of the UK – the country's oldest Jewish community. He is also the Rosh Bet Midrash of The Ḥabura. He studied in Jerusalem at Yeshivat Hazon Ovadia under the tutelage of the former Sephardi Chief Rabbi of Israel, Rabbi Ovadia Yosef. He has an MA in Jewish education. In his capacity as Senior Rabbi, Rabbi Dweck serves as a President of the Council of Christians and Jews, Deputy President of the London School of Jewish Studies, Ecclesiastical Authority of the Board of Deputies of British Jews, and Standing Committee Member of the Conference of European Rabbis. Visit www.SeniorRabbi.com to find out more about his work and initiatives.

Passover is *Zeman Ḥerutenu* — the time of our freedom. And while it commemorates our liberation from Egyptian slavery, it is also a festival *about* freedom. It is aimed at bringing us to an awareness of what it means to be free, as well as to actions that encourage and guide free deed and thought.

One concept that is integral to freedom is time. And we see that issues relating to time run throughout the Exodus narrative as well as the Torah's commandments for Passover.

At the turning point in the Exodus story—the midpoint of the ten plagues—precise timings and temporal contexts are introduced into the manifestation of the plagues. This coincides with Pharaoh's conscious psychological shift in that he openly admits his guilt and iniquity[1] and begins to falter in his resolve to hold his slave population.

Here are some examples from the book of Exodus which refer to the time elements in the plagues:

- *Deber* - Pestilence: "And the Lord fixed a time, saying, 'Tomorrow the Lord will do this thing in the land.' And the Lord did this thing the next day, all the livestock of Egypt died."[2]
- *Barad* - Hail: "'I am about to rain down very heavy hail at this time tomorrow, the like of which there has not been in Egypt from the day of its founding until now.'"[3]
- *Arbeh* - Locusts: "'I am about to bring tomorrow locusts in all your territory...the like of which your fathers did

1 Exodus 9:27
2 *Ibid.* 9:5-6
3 *Ibid.* 9:18

not see nor your fathers' fathers from the day they were on the soil until this day.'"[4]

- *Ḥoshekh* - Darkness: "And Moses stretched out his hand over the heavens and there was pitch-dark in all the land of Egypt three days. No one saw his fellow and no one rose from where he was for three days."[5]
- *Makat Bekhorot* - Death of the Firstborn: "'Thus said the Lord: Around midnight I am going out in the midst of Egypt. And every firstborn in the land of Egypt shall die…' And it happened at midnight that the Lord struck down every firstborn in the land of Egypt…"[6]

Even with the Exodus itself, precise timing was of the essence:

> And it happened at the end of four hundred and thirty years, and it happened on that very day, all the battalions of the Lord went out from the land of Egypt.
>
> *Exodus 12:41*

This sensitivity to the time at hand carried through and became a central aspect of our observance of the commandments and laws of the festival, both in ancient and modern times.

With the *Qorban Pesaḥ* (Paschal lamb):

> And thus shall you eat it: your loins girded, your sandals on your feet, your staff in your hand, and you shall eat it in haste!
>
> *Exodus 12:11*

---

4 *Ibid.* 10:4,6
5 *Ibid.* 22–23
6 *Ibid.* 11:4,12:29

With the *Maṣa*:

> This *maṣa* that we are eating, for the sake of what [is it]? For the sake [to commemorate] that our ancestors' dough was not yet able to rise, before the King of the kings of kings, the Holy One, blessed be He, revealed [Himself] to them and redeemed them, as it is stated (Exodus 12:39): "And they baked unleavened cakes of the dough that they had taken out of Egypt, for it was not leavened, since they had been driven out of Egypt and could not delay…"
>
> *Passover Haggada*

We shall explore some ways that time relates to freedom and how it does so within the law and lore of the holiday.

Level 1: To be free, we must own our own time

On the simplest level, time relates to freedom. It is in our mastery of our own time – having it and owning it – that our basic freedoms function. After all, part of freedom is being at liberty to do what we wish. But underlying that ability is the assumption that we have the *time* in which to do it. If time does not belong to me, if I am not the sole determiner of how I will spend it, I am not at liberty to do with it as I wish, and to that degree I am not free. I must instead follow the wishes of the one who is in charge of it. For this reason, in Jewish law, when a person is paid for work by the hour, (essentially selling one's time to an employer in order to use it to complete work that the employer desires) it is considered theft to do something else during that period. When such employees are engaged in other activities, they are stealing the time that they sold to the employer. When however, our time belongs to us, we are at liberty to act as we wish. We need time in order to be free.

When we were in Egypt, we were slaves to Pharaoh, which meant that he forced us to give up our time to him. It is for this reason (when Moses begins to speak to Pharaoh of a desire for the slaves to leave Egypt and worship the Hebrew God) that Pharaoh responds by saying that they must have too much time on their hands! He corrects this by taking that time away from them.

> And the king of Egypt said to them, "Why, Moses and Aaron, do you disturb the people from its tasks? Go to your burdens!" And Pharaoh on that day charged the taskmasters and overseers, saying, "You shall no longer give the people straw to make the bricks as in time past. They themselves will go and scrabble for straw. And the quota of bricks that they were making in the past you shall impose upon them, you shall not deduct it, for they are idlers! Therefore they cry out, saying, "Let us go sacrifice to our god." Let the work be heavy on the men and let them do it and not look to lying words!
>
> *Exodus 5:4-8*

Pharaoh made the burden of their slavery greater by taking away more of their time. The surplus of time they had by having straw ready for their work was now rescinded and they had to spend more time toiling to gather straw without diminishing the usual quota of bricks. Pharaoh's logic was that, with time that wasn't spent on work, they had the luxury to contemplate possibilities; to entertain alternatives to the tasks that faced them, which is something a slave should never have the luxury of doing. For in possibilities, are choices, and in choices, lies freedom. Pharaoh made sure that they wouldn't have any of it.

Level 2: Time gives us options

The degree to which we are able to choose our own actions, determine our own realities, and achieve our own goals, is the degree to which we can be said to be free people. Time allows for our choices and their outcomes simply by providing for a past and a future. Without time all things would simply be as they are, with no growth, change, processes, decay, or destruction. Time gives us the ability to choose, change, grow, create, and achieve by regularly allowing for the current state to be altered to something else in the future. We must, therefore, be sensitive to what might occur in the future as a result of our choices in the present. In other words, when we are sensitive to consequence (what comes with sequence) and cause and effect, we are able not only to do what we want, but also to achieve future realities that we desire. Simply using our time to do what we want without noticing the future effects of those actions, locks us in to results we might not intend. The truly free person not only wants to do things but also to create things. And for creation, awareness of future consequences is essential. Thus, a free person both needs to have time *and* to be aware of its effects. That means knowing past and future, considering precedents and consequences, and entertaining possibilities that are not now at hand. To do this, one must have command of one's own consciousness, creativity, and attention.

Moses' task was not only to free the slaves physically, but also mentally. Their minds needed to get used to considering consequences and determining the difference between situations of past, present, and future. God's first step in this direction was to give commandments that aimed to support this. One of the first and most central was a command to bake and eat *maṣa*:

> And this day shall be a remembrance for you, and you shall celebrate it...Seven days shall you eat *maṣot*. The very first day you shall

> expunge leaven from your houses...And you shall keep watch on the *maṣot*...For on this very day I brought out your legions from the land of Egypt.
>
> *Exodus 12:14-15, 17*

Baking *maṣa* requires "keeping watch." A peculiar legal requirement of *maṣa* is that it must be made with grains that can become *ḥameṣ*. In other words, if it cannot become *ḥameṣ*, it cannot be made into *maṣa*. This, of course makes the process of baking *maṣa* "perilous" if the dough is left too long without baking it, it will rise and go from being encouraged as a *miṣva* to being severely prohibited!

> One only fulfills the obligation of eating *maṣa* if he ate it from one of the five species [of grain], as it is stated (Deuteronomy 16:3), "You shall not eat *ḥameṣ* upon it; for seven days you shall eat *maṣot* upon it": One fulfills his obligation if he eats *maṣa* [from] things that come to being leavened. But he does not fulfill *maṣa* [with] other things...
>
> *HaRaMBa"M, Laws of Ḥameṣ and Maṣa 6:4*

What is the difference between *ḥameṣ* and *maṣa*? Time. This means that fundamental to baking *maṣa* is attention to time. *Maṣa* is, among other things, a training of sorts — a calling of the distracted, encumbered human consciousness, to pay attention. It is basic training for free thought.

> "And you shall keep watch on the *maṣot*."
>
> *Exodus 12:15*

With the *maṣa*, God commands us to stop thinking like slaves and start thinking like free people by insisting that we learn to focus on time, on consequence, on past and future. To be free means to be fully conscious of reality and its possibilities and, when we are, to choose to act in ways that create the most viable and beneficial circumstances for ourselves and the world.

Level 3: Meaning and value only exist in time

There is yet a deeper layer in the relationship between time and freedom. Central to freedom is our ability to ascribe value to things. Without value, I am left with no gauge as to why any action matters over another, and for that matter, why any outcome would matter over another. Without value, my ability to choose between options is trivial – I am doomed to wade through an endless sea of miscellany which, inevitably, leads to nothing but fatigue and despair. By definition, it is only with value that the notion of choice, and therefore freedom, become relevant and meaningful. But how do I determine the meaning of something? It is often a complicated endeavour, but it is never without the awareness of time.

It is in our awareness of time that meaning manifests for us in the world because it is only in *lacking* – what a thing is missing – that we perceive any meaning at all. But these negations, or awarenesses of non-being (what something is not) are not inherent in objective reality, but judged within the consciousness of the human mind in its awareness of time.

If, for example, in my fulfilment of the Torah's charge to watch the *maṣot*, I look to see if my dough has fermented and become *ḥameṣ*, it is because I consider it possible that it is not yet *ḥameṣ* and may only be so in the *future*. A *maṣa* can only be *not-ḥameṣ* for a consciousness that experiences a potential *maṣa* in time in the mode of *not yet being what it will be*. And when dough is not yet baked, the *maṣa* (or *ḥameṣ*) that it can be exists only for consciousness; the dough has a *maṣa/ḥameṣ*-like future only for consciousness. In itself, however, the dough lacks nothing. It is what it is, and is always so when divorced from a conscious mind temporally judging it — knowing what it was and what it can or will be. Consciousness always introduces lack, negations, or non-being into the world to make sense of it and to introduce purpose to it.

Now this does not mean that things do not change over time outside of my consciousness. Of course they do. But they are never anything other than what they are in the present. There is no consciousness to recognise what it was or what it might be. And therefore, there can be no meaning in it. For as described, meaning only exists in what a thing lacks which only exists in human, temporal perception. Hence, I can adhere to the Torah's charge to watch over the *maṣa-dough* with knowledge of what it might become if I do not intervene and bake it before it rises.

What something is, always is flanked by what it was and what it will be, and these states are superimposed upon the present to establish its meaning and value. I know meaning because I know time.

All of this is packed into the simple baking task that we are commanded to engage in before we even leave Egypt. Take the grain, make the flour, knead the dough, do NOT let it rise, bake it, eat it. When unpacked, all we have mentioned is present in it, and on a level of action, we come to ignite the full nature of human awareness that is the key to our free lives. To a lesser degree, if we do not bake them, but only eat them, we at least are aware of how they came to be *maṣot* — and that brings us to freer thought.

Time is precious. How we spend it is how we spend our lives. To be free is not only to do what we want, but also to create and become what we want. For all of it, we need time. We must have it, know it, and be conscious of it. By telling the story of Pesaḥ and performing the *miṣva* of *maṣa* — the two remaining biblical commandments of the festival — we learn the lessons through experience and instil them into our minds and hearts.

✦

"Imagine That!"[1]

Rabbi Dr. Samuel Lebens

Rabbi Dr. Samuel Lebens is a research fellow in the philosophy department at the University of Haifa, and a dynamic Jewish educator. He has studied at Yeshivat Hakotel, Yeshivat Hamivtar, and Yeshivat Har Etzion. He holds a Ph.D. in philosophy from Birkbeck College (University of London), and held post-doctoral positions at the University of Notre Dame and Rutgers. Rabbi Dr. Lebens is the author of *Principles of Judaism*, published by Oxford University Press.

---

1 This paper is based upon two of my previous academic publications, summarised and stitched together into (I hope) a cohesive and meaningful whole. Those two articles are: *"The Epistemology of Religiosity: An Orthodox Jewish Perspective,"* in *International Journal for Philosophy of Religion*, 74 (2013):315-332, and *"Defining Religion"* in *Oxford Studies in Philosophy of Religion*, volume 10 (Oxford: Oxford University Press, 2022). Many of these ideas are also explored in my book, *The Principles of Judaism* (Oxford: Oxford University Press, 2019).

"We were slaves in Egypt," we tell ourselves and our children each Seder Night, "and the Lord our God took us out from there with a strong hand and an outstretched arm." Luckily, I have no problem reading those words. I believe that they are true.

But then we read, "If the Holy One, blessed be He, had not taken us out of Egypt, then we, our children, and our children's children would have remained slaves to Pharaoh in Egypt." That is where my problem begins.

Do we *really* believe that many thousands of years after the fact, we would still have been slaves to Pharaoh? There *is* no Pharaoh. I lose count of how many revolutions and coups there have been in modern Egyptian history. Do we really believe that, had there been no Exodus from Egypt, we'd still be slaves to Pharaoh? Do we really believe that, had we stayed enslaved, the only political institutions in the history of man to have lasted for that many millennia would have been the Pharaonic ones, which would still be going strong?

My problem is easily solved.

Later in the *Haggada*, we read that "In every generation, a person is obligated to regard himself as if he had come out of Egypt." *As if*. The task is not to believe; the task is to make-believe.

It's important to the Sages that we don't just believe in a historical claim about our ancestors. It is, of course, important that we believe it, but it is not enough. We are also called upon to imagine that, had it not been for Divine intervention, we *ourselves* would be slaves to Pharaoh. To ask whether that's true, it seems to me, is to miss the point. We are not really asked to believe it. We are asked to imagine it. We are asked to pretend.

A similar question, with a similar answer, can be asked about RaMBa"M's ruling:

> Throughout the entire year, a person needs to view both himself and the entire world as if they were equally balanced between merit and sin. If he performs one sin, he tips his balance and that of the entire world to the side of guilt and brings destruction upon himself. [But,] if he fulfils one commandment, he tips his balance and that of the entire world to the side of merit and brings deliverance and salvation to himself and others. As it is said (in Proverbs 10:25): "A righteous man is the foundation of the world." [i.e.] he, who acted righteously, tipped the balance of the entire world to merit, and saved it.
>
> *Hilkhot Teshuba 3:4*

It is a powerful image, but it is not *literally* true. Sadly, from time to time, we sin. And when we do, neither we nor the world in which we live are destroyed (at least not literally).

Some of commentaries on this law of RaMBa"M construct elaborate descriptions of when exactly the judgements of various types are made for individuals, for the countries in which they live, and for the world, and how that order is consistent with the cosmological knife-edge upon which the Rambam seems to imply we constantly walk.

But perhaps that elaborate story misses the point. RaMBa"M says that we have to view ourselves *as if* we and the world are equally balanced – whether or not we are. We must view ourselves *as if* the world will come to an end, or that the world will be saved, depending upon what we do right now – whether or not it will. RaMBa"M is not asking us to believe anything in this halakha. He is asking us to make-believe.

Make-believe is not just for children. One of my favourite examples comes from the neuroscientist V. S. Ramachandran. He is the first physician to have cured the pain of amputees' phantom limbs. Phantom hands are often clenched so tightly that the phantom fingers and fingernails inflict unbearable pain upon the phantom palm. Many of these patients are unable to escape the pain because their phantom fists are paralysed in this eye-watering clench.

Ramachandran discovered a surprisingly low-tech solution. He got his patients to put their remaining hands into a box, mimicking the position that they felt their phantom hands to be in. Inside the box was a mirror. When the patient looked down, he didn't merely see his actual hand; he saw its reflection as well. This looked just like seeing his actual hand *and* his phantom. By slowly opening his only *real* hand, he could make it look as if he was opening both of his 'hands'. And, sure enough, this deceived the brain into thinking that the phantom hand had opened. This relieved the pain.[1]

These patients were quite sane. They knew that they only had one real hand. They knew that the box contained a mirror, but the illusion was all the brain needed to behave appropriately in the real world. I once asked a neuroscientist what might happen if the patients, with their hand in the box, were to repeat, like a mantra, "It's just a mirror! It's just a mirror!" It would be unethical to test what would happen, since – in the opinion of the expert I asked – there is a good chance that such a chant would ruin the therapy. Even though the patients know that it is just a mirror, it is

1 V. S. Ramachandran & S. Blakeslee, *Phantoms in the brain: Probing the mysteries of the human mind* (New York: William Morrow Paperbacks, 1999).

important for them not to focus too centrally on that fact. Rather, they have to suspend their disbelief, and only if they do that can they reprogram their brains to better track their reality.

Recently, I sought to come up with a definition of "religion."[2] It is a difficult thing to do, because the human phenomenon of religion is just so broad that it becomes a challenge to find any common denominator. Most religions believe in the super-natural, or God, or gods, but not all do. So, what else might they all share in common, not shared by non-religions?

Most scholars of religious studies have been resigned to the fact that religion itself is not a single phenomenon that admits of a rigorous definition. Instead, it is something like a patchwork of inter-related but quite different phenomena, with no single thread uniting them all. Swimming against that tide, I have suggested that a definition can be found, but that in addition to the centrality of faith, which all religions seem to demand, and in addition to the centrality of community, which all religions seem set upon creating and sustaining, a communal system of thought and practice cannot be religion until it deliberately engages the imagination.

Most religions have a central place for certain stories. To engage with a story, even if it is literally true, is, first and foremost, to engage one's *imagination*. Indeed, there is neurological research to suggest that we use the same regions of our brain when witnessing an event of type *X*, as we do when

2 See Rabbi Dr. Samuel Lebens, *Defining Religion*.

we read or hear a *story* about an event of type *X*.[3] In other words: to read or listen to a narrative is to engage in a sort of offline mental simulation of witnessing the events described.

But it is not just the centrality of *stories* in religious life that calls for imaginative engagement. Zen Buddhism tends to denigrate the role that stories and narrative should play in our religious lives, but its central meditative practice, known as *zazen*, could be characterised as a very minimalistic and intentionally sparse form of imaginative engagement: you have to imagine that *you are your breath.*

Sometimes a religion will invite us to imagine ourselves, or something around us, in what can only be called a literally true light. According to Rabbi Samson Raphael Hirsch, for example, we are not simply commanded to believe that God exists, we have to *view ourselves* as living in a world in which God exists. The idea is constantly to *see ourselves* as his creations.[4]

We *do* live in a world in which God exists. We *are* God's creatures. But that does not mean that we automatically view ourselves as living in such a world, or as His creatures. When we are asked to imagine ourselves, or something around us, in a *true* light, I would call it '*attentive-seeing-as.*' One does not believe that one is making something up – but that one is trying to *attend* to something that is all too easily ignored. It is as if one is engaging one's imagination in order to see the world *more accurately*, in accordance with what one believes.

---

3 See, for example, R. Marr, "The neural bases of social cognition and story comprehension," *Annual Review of Psychology*, 62 (2011): 103-134, and K. Oatley, "The mind's flight simulator," in *The Psychologist*, 21 (2008): 1030-1032.

4 See R. Hirsch's commentary to the first of the Ten Commandments, in *Parshat Yitro*.

If I am right, then you can believe that the world was created by God, and you can believe that the Israelites were freed from Egypt thousands of years ago. But belief alone is not sufficiently absorbing to count as true religiosity. Every religion demands imaginative engagement. Judaism is no exception. Fine, you may believe that God created the world, that he judged us, and that we were freed from Egypt thousands of years ago. But do these beliefs shape you? And how can you ensure that they do?

Until a person switches on his imagination, true religiosity hasn't yet begun. By using your mind's eye, you can move from *believing* that the world was created by God to *seeing it* as a creation of God. Using your mind's eye, you can move from believing that the Israelites were freed from Egypt to viewing yourself as a member of a liberated people. These things are true, but they require the engagement of the mind's eye to be attended to.

Moreover, sometimes the only way to bring our actions into conformity with our ideology – the only way to shape our actions so that they accurately reflect the contours of the ethical universe in which we live – is to engage with forms of make-believe that *aren't* literally true.

The world will not be destroyed the next moment that you sin. The world will not be saved from disaster with a single solitary *miṣva*. But what happens to us if we try to view our situation *as if* these things were true? If you walk around constantly trying to see yourself as personally liberated by God, seeing all other people in the world as comrades suffering modern day forms of slavery, and if you empathise with them because you were once where they were — then your imagination will be shaping you to act in conformity with the will of God.

The Seder Night can only unleash its full religious potential if we bring our imaginations to the table. Are we indignant at the plight of the oppressed? If we are not, and to the extent that we are not, I would suggest that we have not succeeded in the task of shaping our reality, with our mind's eye, in conformity with the Halakha, that we are obliged to view ourselves as if we were personally liberated from slavery. It is not an easy task. It is the work of a lifetime.

✦

Four Cups of Wine and the Disappearing Blessings?

Rabbi Yamin Levy

Rabbi Yamin Levy is the Senior Rabbi at the Iranian Jewish Center / Beth Hadassah Synagogue in Great Neck, NY. He is the founder and director of the Maimonides Heritage Center based in Israel and New York. He has authored and edited several books and published extensively in English, Hebrew, and Catalan. He published an award-winning novel entitled *Sababa* that deals with the Israeli Arab conflict. Rabbi Yamin Levy has an active YouTube channel and corresponds via email with a learning community around the world.

> I shall lift up a cup of salvations, and I shall call out in the name of the Lord.
>
> *Psalms 116:13*

In one of his mystical visions recorded in what remains of his diary *Maggid Mesharim,* Rabbi Yosef Qaro speaks of his ambition to unify the Jewish people under one universally accepted law. He later went public with his grand vision in his introduction to the *Bet Yosef* where he pledges to resolve fundamental disputes by arbitrating between the three most prominent codifiers of Jewish Law: Rabbi Isaac Alfasi (1003-1103); HaRaMBa"M (1035-1204); and Rabbi Asher ben Yeḥiel, also known as the Ro"Sh (1259-1327). R. Qaro writes as follows:

> And after all this I decided that I would render halakhic decisions and choose between the different views. For this is the goal, that we should have one Torah and one law...I therefore decided that there would be three halakhic pillars upon whose rulings the House of Israel will rest, namely R. Alfasi, HaRaMBa"M, and Rabbenu Asher of blessed memory. I decided that where two of them agree about a particular issue, we would follow their ruling, except for a few cases in which all or most scholars reject that view.
>
> *Introduction to Bet Yosef*

R. Qaro employed democratic principles in legislation, something he believed would resonate with all rabbinic authorities (and all Jewry). His caveat "except for a few cases" refers to the (actually numerous) instances when R. Qaro rules in accordance with the Ro"Sh even though both R. Alfasi and HaRaMBa"M disagree. His ruling regarding how the *miṣva* of the Four Cups of wine is observed at the Pesaḥ Seder is one such example.

The *miṣva* of drinking four cups of wine at the Seder is one of the central features of the *Haggada*. The cups of wine are drunk at various defining moments of the Seder ritual. The Mishna states: "They should not give him less than four cups."[1] The Talmud[2] adds that drinking four cups of wine is an obligation upon all participants: "The sages taught, all are obligated to drink the four cups of wine: men, women, and children." Parenthetically one notices how HaRaMBa"M does not include the children among those obligated to drink four cups of wine: "Each and every one, both men and women, must drink four cups of wine on this night."[3] Religious ritual is not an excuse to inebriate children. While some *Rishonim* as well as *Aḥaronim* qualify the Talmudic charge by suggesting the Talmud only refers to children who have reached the age of *ḥinukh*, which usually can mean as early as age 6 or 7 years old,[4] the RaMBa"M makes no such qualifications. For him children should not be drinking alcoholic beverages.

The importance Ḥazal placed on the four cups of wine at the Seder is evident from the following Rabbinic rulings. Even the beggar must sell his last garment or borrow money to fulfill the *miṣva* of four cups of wine. Even one who hates wine or is harmed by the drinking of wine must extend himself/herself and drink the four cups of wine. Under extenuating circumstances, most halakhic authorities permit one to drink grape juice instead of wine. Even one who has taken a vow not to drink

---

1 *Pesaḥim* 99b

2 *Ibid.*, 108b

3 MT *Ḥameṣ U'Maṣa* 7:7

4 See *Shulḥan Arukh, Oraḥ Ḥayim, siman* 172:15-16, also *Bet Yosef*, where he questions the Ro"Sh and R. Mordekhai. For the age of *ḥinukh* in this context see *Sefer Ḥazon Ovadia*, II, page 5, *siman* 2.

wine must annul his/her vow prior to Pesaḥ in order to drink the four cups of wine. The Halakha requires that even one who cannot read the *Haggada* is nevertheless required to fulfill the *miṣva* of the four cups.[5]

The importance of this *miṣva* is also evident by the numerous and varying reasons given for this commandment. The Jerusalem Talmud[6] teaches that the four cups of wine correspond to the four different verbs of redemption used in Exodus 6:6–7: "I will bring you out; I will deliver you; I will redeem you; I will take you out." Alternatively, the same passage in the Jerusalem Talmud suggests that the four cups of wine correspond to:

- The four cups of wine mentioned in the narrative of Pharaoh's butler
- The four exiles in which the Jewish people will suffer
- The cups of retribution God will force the gentiles to drink in the messianic age
- The four cups of consolation God will offer the Jews after their redemption

For HaRaMBa"M the four cups of wine symbolise freedom and personal autonomy, as he writes:

> In every generation one is obligated to show himself as if he himself had just left the servitude of Egypt…therefore, each person during this night must eat and drink and do so while leaning the way a free

[5] See *Shulḥan Ạrukh, Oraḥ Ḥayim* 472; Ḥakham Ovadia Yosef, *Ḥazon Ovadia on Pesaḥ,* II, chapter 1.

[6] *Pesaḥim* 10:1

> person does, and each person, whether man or woman must drink four cups of wine during this night.
>
> *MT Ḥameṣ U'Maṣa 7:6-7*

A careful reading of the Talmudic text suggests a more basic reason for the four cups of wine. The Mishna states that one is not permitted to drink wine between the third and fourth cup of wine. The Gemara explains:

> Rav Ḥanan said to Raba: From this we can derive that *Birkat HaMazon* requires a cup. He said to him: the rabbis enacted four cups in the manner of freedom so that we perform a *miṣva* over each one of the four cups of wine.
>
> *Pesaḥim 117b*

In other words, each of the four cups of wine accompany a *miṣva* of the Seder and function as indicators, elevating the status of each of the evening's liturgical spiritual movements. Like the recitation of *Havdalah* at the conclusion of Shabbat, or *Birkat Erusin* at a wedding ceremony, the wine functions as a way of elevating the nature of the *miṣva* that is about to be performed. If this is indeed the case one can divide the Seder and the *Haggada* into four distinct sections.

The *Kiddush* section of the *Haggada* announces the holy day and introduces the order of the evening. The *Maggid* section of the *Haggada*, the telling of the story of the Exodus, begins with the filling of the second cup of wine and concludes with its drinking. Then one washes the hands and partakes of the festive meal which ends with *Birkat Hamazon*, at the conclusion of which one drinks the third cup of wine. The last movement of the evening is the recitation of *Hallel* which begins with the filling of the cup of wine and concludes with the drinking of the fourth cup of wine.

HaRaMBa"M mentions a fifth cup of wine:

> One fills a fifth cup and recites upon it the "*Great Hallel*" from *Hodu LaHashem Ki Ṭob* until *Al Naharot Bavel*, this cup is not an obligation like the other cups of wine.
>
> *MT Ḥameṣ U'Maṣa 8:10*

Apparently, he was heir to the tradition that *Hallel* was divided into two parts each of which had its own cup of wine. He was also heir to a universally accepted Geonic tradition that ruled that one must recite a blessing on each of the four cups of wine at each of the four sections of the Seder. This tradition was codified by both R. Alfasi and HaRaMBa"M and it is therefore jarring to read the ruling of R' Yosef Qaro:

> And he drinks the second cup of wine and does not make a blessing before it or after it for we only recite *Boré Peri Hagefen* on the Kiddush and on the cup of *Birkat HaMazon.*
>
> *Shulḥan Ạrukh, Oraḥ Ḥayim, 474:1*

In his *Bet Yosef*, R. Yosef Qaro mentions R. Yiṣḥaq Alfasi's position and adds that R. Alfasi (and presumably all the Geonim in R. Alfasi's camp) regarded each of the cups of wine as an independent *miṣva* and yet he rules in accordance to a tradition observed by the Ro"Sh.[7] Even the ReM"A (Rabbi Moshe Isserles) who normally follows the rulings of the Ro"Sh notes that in Ashkenaz they recite a blessing over each of the four cups of wine at the Seder night.

---

[7] *Teshubot* 14:5

Ḥakham Ovadia Yosef lists the numerous Geonim and Rishonim including HaRaMBa"M and the Tosafists as well as the great Rabbi Eliezer ben Yoel Halevi from Germany (known as Ra'avyah), all of whom recited a blessing on each of the four cups of wine and yet, remarkably, he concludes "we must follow Maran whose rulings we accept."

I, with great trepidation and humility, recite a blessing on each of the four cups of wine during the Seder night – along with the Yemenite community who still continue to adhere to this ancient and universally accepted tradition of the Geonim and HaRaMBa"M.

✦

The Judaeo-Arabic Responsum of "Our Great Rabbi" on Selling *Ḥameṣ*

Professor Y. Tzvi Langermann

Professor Y. Tzvi Langermann earned his Ph.D. in History of Science at Harvard University. After serving some fifteen years on the staff of the Institute of Hebrew Manuscripts in Jerusalem, he joined the Department of Arabic at Bar-Ilan University, where he taught until his retirement in September 2019. His latest books are *Sa'd ibn Mansur Ibn Kammuna, Subtle Insights Concerning Knowledge and Practice* (Yale, 2019), and *In and Around Maimonides* (Gorgias Press, 2021).

M*S Huntington 428*, a precious codex now held by the Bodleian Library in Oxford, contains a significant portion of *Issur ve-Heter*, an unpublished, early comprehensive Sephardi treatise on Halakha. I first identified this treatise in the course of my cataloguing duties at the Institute of Microfilmed Hebrew Manuscripts in Jerusalem, where I was then employed, and published a short description in Hebrew. After the breakup of the former Soviet Union, the Institute obtained films of thousands of precious Jewish manuscripts that had hitherto been inaccessible. I identified among those collections another copy of *Issur ve-Heter*; it too, is incomplete. This second manuscript consists of several disjointed pieces which were bound together by Soviet era librarians and classified as *The National Library of Russia (St. Petersburg), Ms. Evr-Arab I 2901*. Some of its leaves overlap with the text found in Oxford, but there is a great deal of new material there as well.

Having finally retired from teaching, I am now free to devote a significant amount of time to editing and translating this priceless composition. As circumstances allow, I publish sample chapters or significant extracts, hoping—with God's help—to eventually publish the extant text in its entirety. The importance of this treatise is not limited to the many interesting explanations and rulings given by its unnamed author; *Issur ve-Heter* also preserves for us exciting materials hitherto unknown. I offer here one of many important verbatim citations of responsa from Geonim and early Rishonim that are preserved in *Issur ve-Heter*: a responsum from "our great rabbi" concerning the selling of *ḥameṣ*.

Before presenting the responsum, I should first give a more detailed account of the treatise. The extant chapters cover most of the holidays (though the chapter on Shabbat is unfortunately missing) and diverse other topics, such as *'orlah* (the first three years of fruits that are forbidden), circumcision, *ṣiṣit*, and more. The organisation of the chapters differs as well: some present more or less a running commentary on the Mishnah devoted to that topic (e.g., the chapter on Pesaḥ, where the responsum here published is found); others resemble the type of instructions that were included in the earliest siddurim of Sa'ạdya or Ạmram Gaon; still others recall the specialised monographs that were penned by some of the Geonim. The author assembled all of the different topics into a single volume. The book was indeed well-planned: the writing style is consistent throughout, and there are many cross-references. However, the author did not impose a unified structure on all of the different chapters, opting instead to conserve the style of the different genres mentioned above. Comparing *Issur veHeter* to HaRaMBa"M's *Mishneh Torah*, we can better appreciate the uniform organisation that the latter displays throughout all fourteen books—just one of its many astounding accomplishments.

The book is written in Judaeo-Arabic, and the title page announces that the volume contains "the second part of *Issur ve-Heter*." The manuscript provides no information about the name, place, or date of the author. However, after reviewing the names of all the authorities cited — and especially one towering figure who is never mentioned — it became clear that the text predates HaRaMBa"M. A certain "Rabbi Yosef of blessed memory" is mentioned twice, together with "Rabbi Yiṣḥaq" — quite certainly the famous R. Alfasi (RI"F), whose summary of the Talmud is often cited – and I believe that it is reasonable to identify him with R. Yosef Ibn Migash, who succeeded R. Alfasi as the head of the yeshiva in Lucena. Thus, *Issur ve-Heter* seems most likely to have been written by a contemporary of HaRaMBa"M's father, R. Maimon the Judge; his generation – the disciples of R. Yosef Ibn Migash — suffered the brunt of the Almohad invasion, and precious little of their literary output has survived.

My suggestion for the place of writing is more speculative. The book is written in Judaeo-Arabic. However, it reproduces in full a small tract in Hebrew on purging the slaughtered animal of forbidden parts (*niqqur*) written "by one of the outstanding ones"; and that tract exhibits the names of some animal parts in a Romance language, written out also in Hebrew characters. Now the only place I know of where Jews continued to write in Judaeo-Arabic even though they were living in a Christian dominated, Romance-speaking land was northeast Spain. Indeed, though Toledo fell to the *Reconquista* in 1075, Jews living there produced Judaeo-Arabic literature well into the fourteenth century. Hence, with all due caution, I suggest that the book was written somewhere in the northeastern regions of present-day Spain.

The anonymous author informs us that the long chapter on Pesaḥ will be divided into several subsections: "We shall first speak about the *furqān*, I mean the *Haggada*; following that, the prayers; and then I will turn to the obligatory practices, as is my custom in every chapter." The first two sections accordingly are in the style of the early *maḥzorim*, as noted above; the third follows the order of presentation in the tractate *Pesaḥim*, much like the early Mishnah commentaries. The author cites liberally from the Talmud or from R. Alfasi, whose summation of the Talmudic rulings was held to be almost as authoritative as the Talmud itself. He also includes, as is his wont, the full text of an early responsum by "our great Rabbi," to which I shall turn presently. First, though, I must list some pointers concerning the early history of the now widespread practice of "selling the *ḥameṣ*."

The first mention of selling *ḥameṣ* to a non-Jew, with the clear expectation of repossessing the *ḥameṣ* after the holiday, is found in the Tosefta:

> If a Jew and a non-Jew were on a boat and the Jew had *ḥameṣ* in his possession, he may sell it to the non-Jew or give it to him as a gift, and then take it back from him after Pesaḥ, provided that he give it to him as a full-fledged gift.
>
> *Tosefta Pesaḥim 2*

The Tosefta apparently describes a case of extenuating circumstances; the Jew has no other option other than destroying the *ḥameṣ*. (Imagine that the Jew had a valuable consignment of *ḥameṣ* on board, and the ship was delayed for whatever reason and the load could not be sold in port before the holiday.) The *Geonim* and *Rishonim* (halakhic specialists who preceded the *Shulḥan Ạrukh*) accepted this ruling, but they took pains to ensure that it does not become ordinary practice.

Thus Ạmram Gaon, in the only responsum on the subject which certainly preceded the one cited in *Issur veHeter*, endorsed the ruling of the Tosefta with the double stipulation "that there be no *ha'ạramah* (cunning evasion of the law) and that one does not do this regularly in other years."[1] The stipulation banning *ha'aramah* may already have been found in some versions of the Tosefta. *Halakhot Gedalot*, a very early geonic compendium, adds to his citation of the Tosefta the phrase "provided that he is not evading [the law]." Saul Lieberman considers this addition to reflect a different version (*girsa*) of the Tosefta, and he displays a long list of early authorities who add this stipulation. Ạmram Gaon's second stricture is even more explicit in R. Menaḥem Meiri's *novellae* on *Pesaḥim*: "that the Jew is not used to doing this in other years, but rather this situation arose for him just now" — as indeed was the case described by the Tosefta. In other words, the ruling must remain an emergency one-time leniency and should not become common practice.

The responsum cited by *Issur veHeter* is a major breakthrough in the practical application of the Tosefta. As we shall see, "our great rabbi" allows *ha'aramah* and, we may safely assume, recognises that selling *ḥameṣ* to a trusted Gentile is not a rare procedure carried out under extenuating circumstances, but rather common practice. His sole stipulation is that, formally speaking, the sale be legally binding—by the law of the Gentiles as well as in Jewish law. Who is "our great rabbi"? At this point I can only speculate, in line with the suggestions displayed above, and taking into account that the responsum is in Arabic, that it is either R. Alfasi or Ibn Migash. In truth, though, we have no basis for even a tentative identification.

Here follows my translation of the responsum, followed by notes on certain phrases:

1 B.M. Levin, *Oṣar ha-Geonim*, vol. 3 (*Erubin and Pesaḥim*), Jerusalem 1930, p. 21.

> Our great rabbi was asked about the case of someone who possesses *ḥameṣ* or *murri'*, and he evades [the law; *ya'rim.* The technical term of Jewish law remains in Hebrew, even though the responsum is in Arabic.] by selling it to a non-Jew, all the while it remains in the Jew's [private] domain. Is this forbidden or not? He replied: If the sale was final, inasmuch as the non-Jew can take possession of it, and the Jew cannot renege, then it is the property of the non-Jew even though it remains in the Jew's domain; it is considered to belong to the non-Jew. This is permitted, even if he allows him [the Jew] to do with it whatever he wishes after Passover. 'He has simply given him a gift.' However, if the sale is not final according to the law of the non-Jew, such that the Jew may renege and nullify the sale, in that case it is in the [full] possession of the Jew. One is not allowed to derive any benefit from it, and this sale has been to no avail at all.

I have left *murri'* untranslated. The Arabic word corresponds to the Aramaic *muryis* (Latin *muries*). In the Talmud (e.g., *Aboda Zara* 34b) it refers to a pickle made from fish-hash and used as a condiment. There was also a grain-based *muries* which would certainly be considered *ḥameṣ*. Both are mentioned by Isḥāq al-Isrā'īlī, (832-932) of Qairou'an (near present-day Tunis) in his book on foodstuffs; both are strong liquids that are used for therapeutic as well as culinary purposes.[2] The grain-based version (al-Isrā'īlī mentions barley specifically) is probably the most fitting one for the responsum. Evidence may be drawn from *Kaftor va-Feraḥ* (p. 70a), the great halakhic compendium written by Ishtori Farhi (originally from Provence, late 13th-early 14th centuries), who notes the widespread legal evasion (*ha'ạrama*) of the prohibition of possessing *ḥameṣ* by the fictitious sale of "*muries* that derives from grain" to a trusted

2 Isḥāq al-Isrā'īlī, *Kitāb al-Ahgdhiya*, ed. M. al-Ṣabāḥ, Beirut 1412/1992, p. 509

Gentile, on the belief that it will be returned to the Jew after Pesaḥ.

In conclusion, *Issur ve-Heter*, the early, comprehensive work on Halakhah, which is certainly a product of one of the Arabic-speaking Jewish communities — I suggest somewhere in the northeast of present-day Spain — is an invaluable storehouse of early halakhic rulings. Among its treasures is a responsum, which may possibly have been penned by the great R. Alfasi, and which validates the social reality of Jews "selling" *ḥameṣ* to non-Jews before Pesaḥ in the full expectation of regaining that same *ḥameṣ* after the holiday. Even if the Jew had no intention at all of actually transferring the *ḥameṣ* to the non-Jew — and the non-Jew presumably knew this — the sale achieves its purpose of absolving the Jew from the sin of owning *ḥameṣ* during Pesaḥ. The only stipulation is that the sale meets the formal requirements of a transaction under both Jewish and Gentile law.

✦

How is the Sale of *Ḥameṣ* Done?

Dayan Ofer Livnat

Dayan Ofer Livnat is a Dayan of the Sephardi Beth Din of the United Kingdom. A graduate of the Eretz Hemdah Institute for Advanced Jewish Studies in Jerusalem, Dayan Livnat teaches in a number of programs for training rabbis and dayanim, including the *semikha* and *dayanut* programs run jointly by the Montefiore Endowment and Eretz Hemdah. Dayan Livnat previously served in an artillery unit in the IDF and is currently studying for a PhD in Jewish Studies at University College London.

Background

As we all know, it is prohibited to own *ḥameṣ* during Pesaḥ. If someone does not wish to dispose of all the *ḥameṣ* he owns, it is permitted to sell one's *ḥameṣ* to a non-Jew prior to Pesaḥ, and buy it back after Pesaḥ, provided he has full intention to sell it to the non-Jew, and no conditions are attached to the sale.[1] Common custom is to appoint one's rabbi as an agent to sell the *ḥameṣ* to a non-Jew on one's behalf. In this article I will attempt to describe how the rabbi actually goes about selling the *ḥameṣ* to a non-Jew, and various issues that arise surrounding that process.

Normally, the buying and selling of items is not a complicated procedure. The seller gives the item to the buyer, and the buyer gives the seller the payment. If *ḥameṣ* would be sold in this fashion, it would be a very simple procedure. However, the way the sale of *ḥameṣ* is commonly done nowadays, the *ḥameṣ* remains in the seller's home, while the buyer does not provide full payment for it. Additionally, the precise types and amounts of *ḥameṣ* sold are not known. This makes the sale of *ḥameṣ* a challenging procedure.

Removing *Ḥameṣ* from the Home

Several authorities advise that the *ḥameṣ* sold must be removed from one's home. The reason for this is not fully clear, as it is permitted to have in one's home on Pesaḥ *ḥameṣ* that belongs to a non-Jew, provided one is not responsible for it and one puts it aside so that it will not be accidently used. One of the

1 *Tosefta Pesaḥim* 2, 12–13 in Lieberman ed.; RaMBa"M, *Ḥameṣ UMaṣa* 4, 6–7; *Shulḥan Arukh*, *O.C.* 448, 3.

explanations for the instruction that the *ḥameṣ* should be removed from the home is that, since this *ḥameṣ* originally belonged to the Jew, if it is not removed from the home, it does not appear to have been sold, and the Jew may accidentally come to eat from it. The solution in this situation is that, in addition to selling the *ḥameṣ*, one rents out to the non-Jew the cupboards or places where the *ḥameṣ* is located, and in this way it is considered that the *ḥameṣ* has been removed from one's home.[2]

Qinyan – the Act of Acquisition

Halakha requires that the transfer of ownership of an item from one person to another must involve a *qinyan*. A *qinyan* is a defined act by which ownership is transferred. In a normal sale of an item, we have two actions which could be considered the *qinyan*: the lifting of the item by the buyer, termed *meshikha* or *hagbahah*, and the payment for the item, termed *ma'ot.* Regarding a sale by a Jew to a Jew, from the Torah the required *qinyan* is *ma'ot* (payment), while the Ḥakhamim instituted that *meshikha/hagbahah*, the lifting of the object by the buyer, is the required *qinyan*. In a case of a sale' to a non-Jew, there is a dispute amongst the authorities which of the two is the required *qinyan*. If we could do both, then the sale would certainly be effective. However, it is not practical to have the non-Jew go around and lift all the *ḥameṣ* sold to him. Such a payment is simpler to carry out, as one does not need to make full payment for it to be considered *qinyan ma'ot*, and even partial payment is

2 *Terumat Hadeshen* 119; *Shulḥan Ạrukh* ibid; *B"Ḥ, Oraḥ Ḥayim* 448; *Magen Abraham* 448:4; *Ḥoq Ya'ạqob* 448:14; *Mishnah Berurah* 448:12

sufficient. However, as it is not clear that *ma'ot* is an effective *qinyan*, the custom is to do additional forms of *qinyan* to ensure the sale is effective and ownership of the *ḥameṣ* is transferred.[3] The following is a list of the forms of *qinyan* that have been suggested:

- *Ma'ọt* – the non-Jew gives partial payment for the *ḥameṣ*. Even one dollar or pound is sufficient.

- *Agav* – When one acquires land, which may be acquired by payment or by a *shṭar* (a deed), it is also possible to attach to that transaction the transfer of movable items. As mentioned above, we rent to the non-Jew the places where the *ḥameṣ* is located, so that we can attach to the transfer of those places the transfer of the *ḥameṣ* itself. The rental of such places is done by means of payment (partial payment being sufficient as described above) which is then recorded in the contract of the sale of the *ḥameṣ*.

- *Ḥaṣer* – If one owns the property in which an item is located, the item being in his property may also be considered a *qinyan*. Once the non-Jew rents the place or places in which the *ḥameṣ* is located, he may acquire them by *qinyan ḥaṣer* as they are in his property,

- *Sudar* – the non-Jew gives an item such as a handkerchief or pen to the Jew, and in return acquires the *ḥameṣ*.

- *Situmta* – if there is a customary act amongst traders to

3 *Mishna Berurah* 448:17-19.

signify transfer of ownership, such as a handshake in some places, that too is considered a *qinyan.*

- *Odita* – the Jew admits having sold the *ḥameṣ* to the non-Jew, and as this admission is evidence to the sale, it may be considered also as a *qinyan* according to some authorities.[4]

As there are various disputes regarding the effectiveness of all of these *qinyanim* in the sale to a non-Jew, a rabbi will normally do all or many of them with the non-Jew to ensure the sale is effective.

Setting the Price and Detailing the *Ḥameṣ*

Normally, for a sale to be valid, a price must first be agreed upon. Without a set price one is not considered to have full intent for the sale, as the most critical component is unknown. Even if a price is fixed, if one does not have some rough idea of what one is buying, it is also not considered to have full intent for the purchase, as one does not know if the value of the items is equivalent to the set price. For example, HaRaMBa"M writes that if one sells the contents of a sealed box, that is not a valid sale, as the buyer is clueless as to what he is purchasing, and it is akin to a gamble.[5] Therefore, often the sellers will be asked by the rabbi to provide some details on the types of *ḥameṣ* they are selling.

There is a simple solution that solves both issues. Rather than setting a price, the buyer and seller may agree that the price will

4 *Qeṣot HaḤoshen* 194:3. *Meqor Ḥayim* 448:3 disagrees.

5 *Hilkhot Mekhira* 21:3

be determined by three appraisers who will later appraise the value of the items sold.[6] This also solves the issue of the types and quantities of the *ḥameṣ* being unknown, as the buyer is confident that he will only pay the actual value of the items as determined by the appraisers.[7]

Conclusion

The above discussion provides an overview of some of the complications and solutions in the sale of *ḥameṣ* as it is commonly done nowadays. It is due to these difficulties that some authorities advise that, except in a case where significant financial loss is expected, one should avoid the sale of actual *ḥameṣ*. In the case of items *whose status as true ḥameṣ is questionable*, one may be more lenient and rely on the sale. The rabbi who is conducting the sale on behalf of all the sellers must be well-versed and prepared in all the details of the sale to ensure it is effective according to Halakha.

✦

6 *Shulḥan Arukh, Ḥoshen Mishpaṭ* 200:7
7 *Pit'ḥei Teshuba, Ḥoshen Mishpaṭ* 209:1

Biṭul: Nullifying the "What-If" Mentality of Modern *Kashrut*

Rabbi Yonatan Y. Halevy

Rabbi Yonatan Halevy is author of *Yehi Shalom: A Guide to the Laws of Pesaḥ and Kashrut*, the spiritual leader of Kehillat Shaar HaShamayim in San Diego, and the founder of Shiviti. He studied at Ner Israel in Baltimore, and Shehebar Sephardic Centre in Yerushalayim, receiving *semikha* from Rabbi Yaakov Peretz and Rabbi Shelomo Kassin.

Unintentionally, our *Shiviti* Learning Forum has turned into one of the most sought-after Pesaḥ resources online, to the point that we have a dedicated *Pesaḥ Kashrut Forum* just to handle the influx of questions we receive.

What do I mean by unintentionally? It means that if you would have asked me, at the beginning of my Rabbinic career, if I ever intended to enter the arena of *Kashrut* – I would have unequivocally said "no." So how did it all begin?

The story that inspired it all happened when I first moved back to the United States after living in Israel. I found myself in the Kosher[1] section of the local grocery store, shopping for Pesaḥ products for my *Bet Knesset.* Past the Kosher-certified soaps and paper goods, beyond the potato-starch based cookies and cereals, and just beside the snacks laced with cottonseed and palm oils – I walked past the olive oil. Knowing that I had a bottle of olive oil at home, it wasn't the oil that caught my eye, it was the price tag underneath it! Forty-six dollars (roughly thirty-four pounds) for one litre of olive oil! Certainly, there must have been a mistake. I inquired further only to be told that there was no mistake – this was special, *Kosher-for-Passover* certified olive oil!

What happened to the Rabbinic dictum of "the Torah is sparing with the money of Jewish people"?[2]

What makes olive oil specially *Kosher-for-Pesaḥ*? Or even better yet, what makes the uncertified olive oil, sold at a fraction of the cost, not *Kosher-for-Pesaḥ*? Are foods able to be purchased

1 Though the proper Hebrew word is "*kasher,*" I have interchangeably used the more familiar Ashkenazi English variation of the word: "kosher."

2 See *Menaḥot* 76b and *Ḥullin* 49b, only two of the dozens of examples in Rabbinic literature.

for Pesaḥ without a special Pesaḥ certification?

Indeed, in our forum, we clearly permit the consumption of *non-ḥameṣ* foods on Pesaḥ without any special certification. Some of the more common questions we receive are whether we are concerned with trace amounts of non-*kasher* ingredients, or *ḥameṣ* ingredients, or residue found in commercial food production machinery?

To answer questions in order would be in accordance with proper etiquette,[3] but in this case, I feel the need to begin with a brief introduction.

An Introduction

My Rabbi and Teacher, HaRab Yaakov Peretz *shliṭ"a* writes:[4]

> I wish to express here [the] feelings of pain and distress [experienced by] straightforward Torah scholars, who are perplexed by the improper and incorrect paths on which those of our generation walk – these are the excessive opinions, doubts and suspicions which surpass the boundaries of proper justice and truth. There are those who are afraid to follow the *Halakha* as stated in the *Shulḥan Ạrukh* which has been accepted by the Jewish people from generation to generation, for they take into consideration an opinion opposite that of the *Shulḥan Ạrukh*. This leads them to be stringent and add one stringency upon another stringency, resulting in a[n improper] leniency or leniencies which stem from their [improper] stringency. Exactly what Ḥazal saw in their *Ruaḥ HaQodesh* has come true in our days, as they said: "The Torah is destined to be forgotten from Israel"…Rabbi Shimon bar Yoḥai explains: "They wander to ask the

---

3 See *Mishna Abot* 5:7, and as practiced by Ribkah Immenu (see RaSH"I to *Genesis* 24:24).

4 *Emet L'Yaạqob: Orḥot HaRab VeKehillato*, chapter 2, section 2:13

word of Hashem but they will not find it – they will not find clear Halakha and clear Mishnah in one place."[5]

Pesaḥ Products

When most people think of differences between Ashkenazim and Sephardim on Pesaḥ, what usually comes to mind is the Ashkenazi[6] custom[7] of refraining from eating *qiṭniyot* (legumes) on Pesaḥ. Very few know that one of thirteen differences which exist between Ashkenazim and Sephardim in *Hilkhot Pesaḥ*, includes the act of buying products for Pesaḥ without special care being taken to make them *kasher* for Pesaḥ. This far more fundamental difference is found explicitly in the *Shulḥan Ạrukh.*

Maran and RaM"A

We often find that Maran R. Yosef Qaro (1488-1575) permits something and writes so in the *Shulḥan Ạrukh*. More often than not, RaM"A (1530-1572) – while agreeing with Maran on a technical level – is typically more stringent and adds that "in our countries we are strict in this regard."

This perhaps stems from a difference in halakhic philosophy between the two. Maran, and the giants of Sepharad, saw greatness in deciding[8] between two halakhic opinions, often

---

5 *Shabbat* 138b

6 Some Sephardic communities were also accustomed to refrain from eating *qiṭniyot*.

7 On the foundational difference between the seemingly identical Ashkenazi "prohibition" and minority Sephardic "custom" regarding the consumption of *qiṭniyot*, see my video *Kaleidoscopic Kitniyot* on our *Shiviti* YouTube channel.

8 Rabbi Yehuda Leon Ashkenazi ("Manitou") once lamented that contemporary rabbis who offer *"safeq"* in place of *"pesaq,"* contrary to the *Mishnah* (*Abot* 1:16): "Rabban Gamaliel used to say: appoint for yourself a teacher and avoid doubt (*safeq*)."

deciding according to the permissive one whenever possible. In Ashkenaz, however, it appears that RaM"A and other giants of those countries worked very hard to satisfy both opinions[9] – or even several[10] – which led them to make the decision to be stringent[11] whenever possible.

It is also noteworthy to mention that we often find that when RaM"A argues with Maran, he is only stringent *lekhat'ḥila*, on an ideal level. When it comes to cases of *bedi'abad*, after the fact, or of *b'hefsed merubeh*, great monetary loss, RaM"A agrees that the basic *halakha* is in accordance with Maran.

Ḥameṣ Reawakening

There is a dispute among the Rishonim as to whether or not *ḥameṣ* "reawakens" on Pesaḥ. The concept of reawakening greatly affects the outcome of what Sephardim and Ashkenazim can eat on Pesaḥ. Before Pesaḥ, *ḥameṣ* is like any other permitted food, and if it falls into *Kosher-for-Pesaḥ* food, it would be nullified as long as the *Kosher-for Pesaḥ* food is sixty times greater than the *ḥameṣ* which fell into it. If the same scenario would occur on Pesaḥ, even if only a crumb of *ḥameṣ* would fall in, it would make the food absolutely not

---

9 See *Nefesh HaRab*, in which Rabbi Hershchel Shachter explains that his rabbi, Rabbi Joseph Solovetchik, understood this as the *Ḥasidut* of the early "*Ḥasidei Ashkenaz*."

10 It is our opinion that when attempting to follow two opinions, one essentially is creating a third. Consider for example the Ashkenazi custom (see RaM"A to the end of *Yoreh De'aḥ* 289:6) of affixing the Mezuzah slanted, in such a way that it fulfills neither halakhic opinion, yet considered a practice of those who are "scrupulous."

11 Contrary to popular opinion, "stringent" is not "better". For further conversation on this topic, please see the chapter on stringencies in my book, *Yehi Shalom*.

Kosher-for-Pesaḥ. The reason being that *ḥameṣ* is now considered a prohibited food which cannot be nullified, even if the *Kosher-for-Pesaḥ* food amounted to a thousand times more than the *ḥameṣ*.

Some Rishonim were of the opinion that *ḥameṣ* nullified before Pesaḥ can actually "reawaken" on Pesaḥ and cause the food to become completely *ḥameṣ*, while others disagreed. According to Maran,[12] once the *ḥameṣ* is nullified in the food before Pesaḥ, it is no longer able to "reawaken" and make the *Kosher-for-Pesaḥ* food *ḥameṣ*. RaM"A though is of the opinion that *ḥameṣ* is able to be reawakened.[13]

Preserved Food Items

Maran[14] is of the opinion that if dried meat, cheese or fish were salted before Pesaḥ, they are permitted to be eaten on Pesaḥ, even if no special care was taken to make them Kosher-for-Pesaḥ. RaM"A notes that there are those who disagree, and that the custom in Ashkenaz is not to eat such food on Pesaḥ.[15]

Conclusion

As is seen from the above sources, it is clear why Sephardim and those who adhere to the rulings of Maran do not need to

---

12 *Shulḥan Arukh, Oraḥ Ḥayim*, 447:4

13 In his review of my book, *Yehi Shalom*, Rabbi Yehoshua Gerstein added that RaM"A does agree that *ḥameṣ* does not reawaken in certain situations, such as *laḥ b'laḥ*.

14 *Shulḥan Arukh, Oraḥ Ḥayim*, 447:5

15 In his review of my book, *Yehi Shalom*, Rabbi Yehoshua Gerstein noted that if one would wash this meat three times, RaM"A would allow one to eat it.

concern themselves with the stringencies of others on Pesaḥ. We respect those who have a custom to do so, but ask that they respect our Ḥakhamim and refrain from imposing their customs on us.

A Second Look

Truthfully, what I wrote above should suffice to show that it is entirely permissible for Sephardim to purchase *non-ḥameṣ* food products that were not prepared in any special way for *Pesaḥ*. Additionally, it is the way of Mori HaRav Yaakov Peretz *shliṭ"a*, not to bring excess proofs to halakhic opinions, for then it seems that there is a need to prove something.[16] But, since we mentioned buying food products that perhaps may have a problem of traces of *non-kasher* ingredients, it is important for me to briefly discuss the laws of *biṭul* and purchasing food from non-Jews.

A Warning

Before I do so, I must declare that I do not advise any of my *talmidim* to purchase foods that certainly have *ḥameṣ* in them, regardless of the amount! It pains me that those who look for leniencies revel in the words of Halakha when it suits them, but ignore it when it does not appeal to them. We are not looking to make lenient Jews – we are looking to educate wholesome Jews, armed with the knowledge of Torah and

[16] Mori HaRab once shared that if Rabbi Ovadia Yosef would have answered his *Teshubot* as curtly and cryptically as Rabbi Moshe Feinstein, for example, his words would have been treated with more authority.

who overcome laxity with subservience to *HaQadosh Barukh Hu*!

I am coming instead to elucidate the reason why we do not busy ourselves with endless doubts and concerns, even though that should be understood from Maran above. In doing so, I will include Ashkenazi sources so that it cannot be argued – as it often is – that this is permissible only for Sephardim.

Historical Precedent

RaShB"A[17] (1235-1310) writes regarding a food product which used miniscule amounts of *non-kasher* vinegar in its production. RaShB"A ruled that this product would indeed be forbidden, since *Biṭul* only applies when the occurrence is accidental. If it were done intentionally, it is prohibited, whether or not the person doing it is Jewish.

HaRav Yeḥezkel Landau (1713-1793), in *Responsa Nodạ BiYehuda*[18] has a similar *teshuba* regarding an alcoholic drink which incorporated animal meat which wasn't *kasher* in its production process. He ruled that the ingredient was considered nullified and that the final product was permissible for consumption. It is noted that his ruling is in agreement with RaMBa"M (1138-1204) and R"I MiGA"SH,[19] (1077-1141) but contrary to that of RaShB"A. Landau explains that since the *Biṭul* was performed by a non-Jew it is permissible,

---

17 *Teshubot HaRaShB"A*, III, *siman* 214, quoted by Maran in *Bet Yosef* (*Yoreh De'ạh, siman* 144).

18 *Mahadura Tanina, teshuba* 56.

19 The acronym for Rabbenu Yosef Ibn Meir Ha-Levi Ibn Megas, teacher of RaMBa"M.

though if the exact same thing were to be done by a Jew, it would be prohibited.[20]

Biṭul

RaMBa"M writes:

> The Torah forbade only [the use of] a pot that was [cooked with the forbidden substance] on that day. For [in that time,] the flavour of the fat absorbed in the pot had not been impaired. According to Rabbinic Law, one should never cook in it again. For this reason, one should never purchase used earthenware utensils from Gentiles to use them for hot foods, e.g., pots and plates. This applies even when they are coated with lead. If one purchased such a utensil and cooked in it from the second day onward, the food is permitted.
>
> *Mishneh Torah, Ma'akhalot Assurot 17:2*

Maran[21] codifies this *halakha*:

> Any pot which is not *Bat Yoma* is considered [that] its taste is detrimental, and it is does not make forbidden [food cooked in it]. And it is called *"Bat Yoma"* all the time that it has not sat from one moment to another moment that the forbidden thing was cooked in it, and once "from one moment to another moment that the forbidden thing was cooked in it" has passed [i.e. it has sat for twenty-four hours since the forbidden food was cooked in it] it is not called *Bat Yoma*. And if one cooked in it when it was not *Bat Yoma*, the cooked food is permissible for this will be a "giving a detrimental flavor" and this is [only] that [the pot] is rinsed such that there is not any residue on the inside, and if one

---

20 The *Noda BiYehuda* deserves further study, and these few lines do not do justice to a brilliant *teshuba*.

21 See similarly what Maran rules elsewhere in 122:7. See *Igrot Moshe* (*Yoreh De'aḥ* 2:41) who explains that when Maran uses the word "forbidden" there, it is only used to state that it is forbidden to tell the Jew to nullify the *issur* for us, but that the food itself certainly does not become prohibited.

> did not rinse it, it makes things [cooked in it] forbidden and this is like a piece of forbidden [food] that is not detrimental. And there are those who allow even [the food that] one cooked in it before rinsing it.[22]
>
> *Yoreh De'ạh 103:5*

Rabbi Moshe Feinstein explains the above RaMBa"M and Maran in the context of permitting margarine that was produced by a non-Jewish company on *non-kasher* machinery:

> Regarding the law of one who maliciously violated [the words of our Ḥakhamim] and cooked in a pot that was not "*Bat Yoma*", we do not find in the Talmud or the *Poseqim* that [our Ḥakhamim] penalised him and prohibited him from eating the food...and from the RaMBa"M...and the *Shulḥan Ạrukh*...it is implied that even when done maliciously, the food is permitted...This is not like what the *Darkhe Teshuba* quotes in the name of the *Ḥamude Daniel* who prohibits the food, and it is a strange thing to invent a prohibition on his own which is not found in the Talmud and the *Poseqim.*
>
> *Igrot Moshe, Yoreh De'ạh 2:41*

Though this is not exactly the same as a non-Jew nullifying an actual *issur* for us, it is obvious that the similarities are striking, and one can learn that the *bedi'abad* action done by the non-Jew is actually permitted *lekhatḥila* for the Jew at the time of purchase.

Nullification by a Non-Jew

While there are those who prohibit *biṭul* done by a non-Jew, there are an overwhelming number of *Poseqim* who permit this

22 RaM"A adds: "and if there are sixty against that which was stuck to its inside, everyone [agrees that this is] permissible from when the pot is not *bat yoma*. And this is how one acts."

entirely. For deeper insight, please see *Darkhe Teshuba,*[23] who deals with this issue at length.

Be'er Heṭeb[24] states that it is the custom to purchase things which are forbidden *lekhatḥila* but are permitted *bedi'abad*.

Seemingly, *Sha"Kh*[25] prohibits such a circumstance since he claims that the time of purchase is *lekhatḥila*. Though it may seem that way initially, *RaShBa"Sh*[26] explains that it is only prohibited when the non-Jew intentionally performs the action for the Jew, but if not, it is permitted.

MaHaRa"M of Lublin[27] agrees with this *halakha* and adds that even if the Jew were there at the time the prohibited action was being done by the non-Jew, it is still permitted since the Jew did not instruct him to do so.

RaDba"Z[28] disagrees with the above ruling when it comes to *biṭul*, and states that the *biṭul* happens at the time of purchase. His logic is that the Ḥakhamim permitted *biṭul* when it happens in a Jew's home so that he will not lose money, but that they would not allow one to go out and purchase something that had nullified *issur* in it.[29]

Though *Yad Abraham*[30] challenges RaDba"Z, based on *Yad HaMelekh*, who brings numerous refutations against the arguments of RaDba"Z, he did not feel that he should rule

23 *Yoreh De'ạh* 108, footnote 20

24 Quoted in *Darkhe Teshuba*, ibid.

25 *Yoreh De'ạh* 60, footnote 5

26 In his halakhic responsa

27 *Siman* 104

28 In his *Responsa*, III, *siman* 578

29 This fits in well with the ruling of RaM"A in *Yoreh De'ạh* 108. See the *Darkhe Teshuba* (*ibid.*) who shows from other rulings of RaM"A that there is room for leniency in this matter.

30 *siman* 99

against RaDba"Z, since he only prohibited regarding *biṭul* and not other *issurim*.

Ḥ aTa"M Sofer[31] has an interesting case in which he allows one to sell a product to a non-Jew and then purchase it back from him, therefore making the *biṭul* happen while it was in the hands of the non-Jew, relying on MaHaRa"M of Lublin mentioned above.

Regardless, one of our greatest Ḥakhamim, R. Yiṣḥaq Tayeb of Tunis,[32] disagrees with HaRab Yehuda Assad who prohibits this case of *biṭul* in his book *Bet Yehudah*, and permits this for consumption. Most importantly, elsewhere in his writings he proves that RaDba"Z changed his mind and agreed to be lenient even in the case of *biṭul*.

Though I wish to continue and share what Hashem has allowed me to capture in the net of my search, "what the heart desires the time denies" – and I will instead have to suffice with the names of a few more Ḥakhamim who agree with MaHaRa"M of Lublin and permit purchasing foods which were nullified by a non-Jew:

- *Shu"t Bet Shlomo (Oraḥ Ḥayim 97)*
- *Shu"t Ketab Sofer (Oraḥ Ḥayim 87)*
- *Shu"t Ḥomat Yesharim (Siman 30)*

---

31 *Yoreh De'ạh* 82. R. Aryeh Leibush Bolichover in *Shem Aryeh (Oraḥ Ḥayim, siman* 8) agrees.

32 *Ẹrekh HaShulḥan, Yoreh De'ạh* 115:7. *Mori HaRab* once shared with me that the *Ẹrekh HaShulḥan* is always stringent, and therefore when he is lenient, that must be the truth – since he must have been unable to find a compelling reason to be stringent!

Conclusion

As *Mori HaRab* wrote above, the world of *Kashrut* today has become full of "excessive opinions, doubts and suspicions which surpass the boundaries of proper justice and truth." It is our sincere hope to return *Kashrut* to the realm of justice, truth, and normalcy.

Those who wish to be stringent – we allow them to do so! We simply ask them to stay out of our way as we focus less on pots and pans, and more on true *Ạbodat Hashem*. We strive to reach not just purity in our foods, but also in our hearts and minds, so that we may be in awe of Hashem, in order to ultimately reach that lofty level of true love of Hashem. Perhaps this year, instead of focusing on ingredients labels and Facebook posts, we may merit to experience the Divine Encounter that Rabbenu Abraham ben HaRaMBa"M[33] spoke of, when properly focusing on our service of the Creator.

To the beloved members of The Ḥabura, I wish you and your loved ones endless blessings – and may we always rejoice in the study of the Torah together.

✦

33 *Kitāb Kifāyah al-`Ābidīn (HaMaspiq L'Ọbdei Hashem)*

Discussion Points for the *Seder* Night: On Reaching Utopia and Other Misplaced Whims[1]

Rabbi Abraham Faur

Rabbi Abraham Faur is the rabbi of Congregation Ohel David and Shelomo in New York. Rabbi Faur was ordained by Rabbi Mordechai Eliyahu and Rabbi Abraham Shapira. He teaches Talmudic and Rabbinic thinking in accordance with the Andalusian Ḥakhamim, and the teachings of his father, the great Ḥakham Jose Faur *a"h*. Rabbi Faur has also studied various scientific and philosophic disciplines.

---

1 Every year on the 1st night(s) of Pesaḥ, my father, Ḥakham José Faur *a"h*, would mesmerise us all with amazing and insightful discussions regarding the meaning of slavery and freedom. This article continues some of those discussions.

Utopian Societies

A feature of utopian societies is that one is neither allowed to criticise nor scrutinise the ruling class. Like an audience member watching a Marvel's superhero movie, suspending critical judgement is essential.

To prevent critical thinking, and promote subservience to the state, instruments that could be used to break free from state-imposed conventions are suppressed by the political elite.[1] The Bible teaches us that during the Philistine rule over the coastal plains of Israel prior to the establishment of the Kingdom of David, smithing was forbidden, to ensure that the fledgling Jewish state could not produce metallic weapons of war, with which it would defend itself. Similarly, this paper will examine how and why the family unit was suppressed by the Pharaohs of Exodus, as well as by other tyrants. Briefly, as will be examined, the family empowers its members to see-thru and oppose corrupt dictators as well as petty politicians. Such suppression seeks to impede the individual's ability to exercise critical thinking, which is the greatest danger facing demagogues throughout world history. Hence, continued fidelity towards demagogues by abused citizens is ensured, and utopia is maintained in the feeble minds of those same citizens.[2]

This paper will describe what it is specifically that the family unit offers its members, which enables them to oppose the tyrant.

---

1 For a contemporary version of state-endorsed-narratives, cf. Facebook "fact checkers."

2 Surely, the Metaverse will appeal greatly to feeble minds seeking utopia.

The Abolition of the Family

Tyrants and their enablers strive to abolish the family: Lenin, Trotsky, Alexandra Kollontai, Wilhelm Reich, Herbert Marcuse, Marcel Foucault, the Bolsheviks, many Israeli *Kibbutzim*, the Frankfurt School, Mao Tse-Tung, anti-war 60's protestors, Democrat party progressive activists, etc., consistently and actively promoted promiscuity and its flip side, the abolishment of the family.[3] Frederick Engels candidly states that the objective of Marxism is to:

> ...push to abolish all right of inheritance, to end home and religious education, to dissolve monogamy in marriage, to pursue pre- and extra-marital sex, to foster ... the gradual growth of unconstrained sexual intercourse by unmarried women, to nationalise all housework, to shift mothers into factories, to move children into daycare nurseries, to separate children into community collectives apart from their natural parents, and, most of all, for society and the state to rear and educate children.[4]
>
> *The Origin of the Family*

Analogously, the youth movement of Nazi Germany sought to ensure the future of the Nazi party by undermining the authority of parents. Hence, parents were denounced by their children if they did not properly submit to the Reich.[5] The strategy was clear: to weaken the bonds between parents and their children, and thereby augment the government's ability to dominate and control these children.

---

3 *The Federalist*, "Americans Buy into Marxist Family Planning," 29 June 2015

4 *The Federalist, ibid.*

5 *The History Channel*, "How the Hitler Youth Turned a Generation of Kids into Nazis"

The French philosopher, Charles Fourier, represents the anti-family ideology of dictators, when he emphasises the importance of giving in to one's passions, whatever these may be.[6] In the modern era, promoting promiscuity, as Hollywood has unabashedly done for decades, represents a sinister attempt to weaken people's adherence to family values and replace these with a deviant wokeness, which creates perfect and submissive citizens.[7] Tyrants and their sponsors recognise that promiscuous people with weak family bonds make intellectually feeble and submissive citizens of the state. This is the reason that tyrants, as a strategic matter, seek the abolishment of the family structure. Woke ideology is not merely a reflection of this strategy, but is an intentional attempt to promote values that contradict the traditional family structure, analogous to Charles Fourier's stated goals.

The Jewish *Bayit*

The first verse of Exodus states: "[T]hese are the names of the children of Israel coming to Egypt together with Ya'ạqob, every man arrived with *beto*." *Beto* is a synonym, which generally means house, but more specifically, in the context of this verse, means family. Thus, every man entered Egypt together with, and as the head of a family. This meant that every Jewish child

---

6 *Rational Action*, "Charles Fourier and the Gravity of Passions in the Wake of Revolution"; *Wikipedia*, "Charles Fourier"

7 In the October 13, 2014 episode of the Disney TV show, *Once Upon a Time*, Mulan is shown having romantic feelings towards Aurora. These romantic feelings are completely marginal to the story. They were artificially inserted by Disney for the sole purpose of promoting promiscuity. It matters little to Disney that *Once Upon a Time* is a show produced primarily for a younger non-adult audience.

in Egypt was raised by a mother and a father.

In Exodus 1:21, Hashem rewards the Jewish midwives for failing to comply with Pharaoh's instructions and tellingly, "made for them *batim*," which is the plural form of *bayit,* and which in the context of that verse, also means families. Hence, for defying the order of the Pharaoh, which was that the midwives destroy the Jewish families (by killing all male babies), God rewarded the midwives by giving them their own families.

It may be instructive to consider more closely the connection between *beto* in verse 1 and *batim* in verse 21. A defining characteristic of tyrannies is the control of information that the public may be exposed to. The narrative that the government voices (or permits to be voiced) is closely crafted and controlled by the ruling elite. For example, Soviet law stipulated that the Communist Party was to have control over all printed media in the USSR. Typewriters were officially registered with the Soviet government, and printouts were collected and stored with the secret police so that if a dissenting opinion was published, the author could be properly identified and punished.[8] At the same time, mass destruction of pre-revolutionary material was enforced, while "special collections" (*spetskhran*), of incorrect information, were only accessible for research purposes, by special permission granted by the KGB.[9] Moreover, "libraries were registered and an inspectorate set up to ensure compliance; items regarded as harmful were weeded from the collections. Books that were considered harmful...[which] failed to promote the worker's class

8 *Must Read Alaska*, "Smuggled Typewriters and the Parallels Between Soviet Socialist Regime and America in 2021"

9 *Wikipedia*, "Censorship in the Soviet Union"

consciousness and willingness to work hard, contained religious propaganda and pro-tsarist ideas" were banned.[10]

A person raised in the USSR, or in Egypt under the Pharaoh,[11] would have no way of knowing that there is an alternative to the hardships imposed by the ruling class. Indeed, the notion that government-imposed utopia is anything but delightful, was an affront to all decent citizens. In tyrannies, the intelligentsia are the first to be emotionally destabilised by those impudently questioning government-imposed orthodoxy.[12] In this kind of environment, perhaps one of the few alternative sources of information, and of right *vs.* wrong, is the family. This is because the family is not only separate from the state but draws upon traditions and teachings that may pre-date the state. Within the family, wisdom, which would normally be hidden from citizens of the state, continues to be passed on from generation to generation, and from person to person.

A Shared Theme of Pesaḥ and Ḥanuka

In the days of the Maccabees, the national religious leaders of the Jewish people, i.e. the priests serving in the Temple, as well as the political ruling class, abandoned the laws and wisdom of

[10] *Ibid.*

[11] ...as well as perhaps in some contemporary western democracies.

[12] Cf., the vigilant cancellation by tech monopolistic overlords of those hurtfully questioning the legitimacy of government mandated vaccines. Western intelligentsia and university folk astutely (and prudently) ignore Sec. 1 of the Nuremberg Code (1947), which states that "The voluntary consent of the human subject is absolutely essential" for any experimental medication. Hence, the occasional judicious and eminently sane rabbis who promote statism by forbidding unvaccinated from joining religious services. "Show us your papers!" is no doubt a delightful way to commence Shabbat morning services.

the Torah in favor of enlightened Greek culture and nationalism. Because the nationalistic values of the Greeks were in opposition to the nationalistic values of Israel, it was up to Jewish families, operating within the four walls of their homes, to oppose the new-fangled Hellenisation, and to pass on the values and teachings of the Torah, and of Jewish nationhood, to the next generation. Remarkably, while the political and spiritual elite of the city of Jerusalem adopted Hellenism, Jewish *batim*/families continued to pass on the traditions and values of the Torah. Jewish boys and girls raised within the *bayit,* were unimpressed with naked athletes performing in public stadiums (perhaps resembling soiled chimps fighting over a rotten banana).[13]

Because they were raised in *batim,* Jews throughout history preferred the sublime beauty of a verse in Job, or perhaps the eternal wisdom of a verse in Proverbs, to a Gentile world featuring naked athletes, raving lunatic politicians,[14] and romantic Hollywood flicks.

In recognition of the essential role of the Jewish family/*bayit,* in pushing back against the attempted Hellenisation of the Jewish people, and in preserving the law and wisdom of the Torah, Ḥakhamim instituted the *miṣva* of lighting a *ner,* i.e. an oil candle (or candles), on Ḥanuka. As will be seen, the lighting of the Ḥanuka candles by every Jewish family, is analogous to the lighting of the Menora in the Temple by the *Kohanim.* To appreciate the significance of this, it should be noted that the evening lighting of the Menora, was one of the most transcendent and spiritually uplifting services in the Temple.

---

13 Cf., "love" scenes in Hollywood movies and TV shows.

14 Cf., Academic gender identity studies programs, in most USA Universities.

The privilege of lighting the Menora was reserved especially for the *Kohanim*, while others would only be allowed to witness the lighting from afar. The luminous glow of the gold Menora, against the darkness of the Jerusalem night, symbolised the iridescent wisdom of the Torah, shining from the Temple towards all of Israel. Without this radiance, Israel would be in the worst darkness possible: ignorance of God and of His laws.

With the Maccabean defeat of the Greek armies in Jerusalem, the Menora in the Temple was reconsecrated. The reconsecration of the Menora was memorialised by the transformation of this event (as well as the concomitant miracles that took place) into the *miṣva* of *Ner Ḥanuka*. This *miṣva* has a unique feature: *misvot* are usually compulsory upon either individuals (such as daily prayer) or upon the nation (such as daily sacrifices). In stark contrast, as the Talmud states, the *miṣva* of *Ner Ḥanuka* is compulsory as follows: *"ner ish u'beto."*[15] Literally, this means that the obligation to light the *ner* Ḥanuka is imposed upon "every man with his family." The last two words "*ish u'beto*," describing who is obligated to light the *Ner Ḥanuka* , are the exact words used to describe the Israelites entering Egypt: "*ish u'beto,*" every man with his family. This cannot be a coincidence. To begin with, the *miṣva* of *Ner Ḥanuka* is compulsory upon the *bayit,* i.e. the family, and not upon the individual. Because the *miṣva* of *Ner Ḥanuka* obligates the family and not the individual, the father's role, as the head of the family, is to ensure that his family lights the *Ner Ḥanuka* in a timely fashion (with or without him). Hence, if a father arrives home after his family has already lit the *Ner Ḥanuka*, he has no personal obligation to light a *ner*; nor is he obligated to

[15] *Shabbat* 21b

even see a *ner*. Similarly, as there is no personal obligation to light a *ner* on Ḥanuka, a young adult who is away from his parent's home on Ḥanuka (perhaps dorming in school), is exempt from lighting a *Ner Ḥanuka*. It follows that if a father were to arrive home well after sunset during each of the eight nights of Ḥanuka, while on each night, his family lit the *ner* Ḥanuka in his absence, he cannot be faulted for not having performed the *miṣva* of *Ner*. To be precise, because as an individual, he has no personal obligation to light the *Ner Ḥanuka* , but rather, as the head of the family, his obligation is to instruct his family to light the *ner*, by instructing his family to light the *Ner Ḥanuka* in his absence, he has completely discharged his duties in regard to this *miṣva*.

Requiring the family, and not the *Kohanim*, to light the *Ner Ḥanuka*, appears to run contrary to traditional decorum: as it is only the *Kohanim* who light the Menora in the Temple, the *Kohanim* would expect to receive some preferential treatment with respect to the *miṣva* of *Ner Ḥanuka*. Why did the Ḥakhamim decide to give the family/*bayit* the honor of lighting the *Ner Ḥanuka* – symbolising the lighting of the Menora in the Temple – symbolically displacing the traditional role of the Kohanim? We may infer that the Ḥakhamim intentionally displaced the Kohanim because, during the era symbolised by Ḥanuka, the *Kohanim* failed to serve as credible spiritual leaders, insomuch as they promoted a foreign set of values and attempted thereby to displace the Torah and *miṣvot*. With the failure of the *Kohanim*, the *bayit*/family continued its adherence to the wisdom of the Torah and the fulfillment of the *misvot*. For this reason, on Ḥanuka, the Kohanim are themselves displaced by the members of the family, and the Temple — in Hebrew,

Bet HaMiqdash, which literally means the *house* of the holiness — is replaced by the physical home/*bayit*/family. At times such as this, the following cry resounds throughout the land: "every man, O Israel, return to your tent."[16]

The profound lesson of Ḥanuka is that the continuity of the Torah and *misvot* do not require proper Jewish leaders. When Jewish leadership fails, Jews continue the light of the Torah within the confines of the *bayit*.

Significantly, the *origins* of the role of the *bayit* in Jewish society, are to be found in the story of the Exodus from Egypt. As subjects of Tyrant Pharaoh, who sought the physical and mental subjugation of *all* of his patriotic citizens, Jews were expected to fall in line, and be obedient. This obedience included not only physical work but also mental submission to the dual principle that: (i) the Pharaoh has the right to force them to work for him, and (ii) they should perform this work submissively without voicing opposition to or thinking ill of the system that oppresses them.

Jews would have none of this, and continued transmitting the stories of Abraham, Yiṣḥaq and Ya'ạqob to their children, dreaming of a return to the land of Israel as a free people. When darkness overtakes the land, as it did in Egypt, "for all of Israel, there was light in their abodes!"[17] Because of this light, the Jewish midwives recognised Pharaoh's order to them — kill male babies! —for the darkness and depravity that it was. By refusing to submit to this darkness and depravity, they effectively allowed the light of the Torah to shine brightly in the Jewish homes.

---

16 Chronicles II 10:16.

17 Exodus 10:23

In answer to the question asked above, the relationship between *beto* in verse one of Exodus, and the *batim* made for the midwives in verse twenty-one, is clear. Because the midwives were themselves raised in *batim,* they had the intelligence and fortitude to say no to Tyrant Pharaoh. In reward for their rejecting the power of the dictator for the wisdom taught to them in the *bayit,* God gave the midwives their own *batim,* thus allowing them to continue teaching the wisdom of God to their own children!

The idea of *bayit* is perpetuated by the *miṣva* of the Paschal sacrifice, which (like the *Ner Ḥanuka*) may not be brought by an individual or by the nation, but rather by the extended extra-family unit called the *ḥabura.* However, this will need to be the subject of a further study on the matter.

The Secret Weapon that Destroys Tyrants

It would not be without merit to address, if only partially, what is it that Jewish *batim* teach its members that allows them to see that the emperor is naked. Perhaps the most fundamental teaching that the Jewish *bayit* provides to its members is consonantal-alphabetic reading.[18] HaRaMBa"M codifies that the minimum educational obligation of a father towards his son is to teach him to be able to read the entire written Torah properly.[19] Failure to do so is a dereliction of duty. Significantly, because the holy texts of the Hebrews contain no vowels or prosodic marks, Jewish consonantal reading requires the young

---

18 For a full discussion of this topic, see Jose Faur, *The Horizontal Society: Understanding the Covenant and Alphabetic Judaism* (Academic Studies Press: Boston 2008), pp. 13-20.

19 *Mishneh Torah, Hilkhot Talmud Tora* 1:8

child/reader to supply both vowels and punctuation marks. Hence, children are taught at a young age to analyse and combine letters precisely, while concurrently joining words to create sentences, ultimately attaining a precise reading of the text. Subsequently, the reader learns how to offer a proper etymological and phonological interpretation of the text.

Quite simply, because Jews were experts at consonantal-alphabetic reading, they also knew how to properly read the world around them. While gullible analphabetic people are easily manipulated by political elites, submissively adopting (and even vociferously defending) the narratives that are fed to them, consonantal-readers have the ability to read matters precisely and correctly; thusly, they reject contrived-fully-transparent-narratives, even if these are promoted by famous people. Jews read the society around them, and concluded that Pharaoh is not a God, and consequently, that being a slave of the Pharaoh does not give meaning to one's life.

In contrast to the Jewish emphasis on precise reading of written texts, the Greeks looked down upon writing, since they considered it to be an impediment to real knowledge and understanding.[20] Writing may be useful as "an aid for memorisation, but it always falsified and distorted the original spoken word." Ḥakham Faur writes that "[T]o the Greek mind, writing is some sort of counterfeit, at best to be tolerated as an aid for memorisation, but always falsifying and distorting."[21] Disapproval of written texts excludes punctilious readers and

---

20 See my article "Ignoring the Writing on the Wall: Semiology vs. Metaphysics," *Hakira, the Flatbush Journal of Jewish Law and Thought,* (XXXI, winter 2022), pp. 89-105.

21 *The Horizontal Society: Understanding the Covenant and Alphabetic Judaism*, p. 15

promotes analphabetic and submissive thinking.

The above is related to what I call "submissive reading." Submissive reading starts with an author who asserts dominance over the readers by using the text to convey a fixed and specific message. What is important is the fixed message intended by the author; hence, the only good reader is the submissive reader. A submissive reader obediently reads the text through the mind of the author and specifically as intended by the author. Perhaps a written text can then be compared to a glass window, which looks towards the original mind of the author, while he wrote the words. The job of the submissive reader is to look through this window and learn what exactly the author was thinking of at the time that he wrote the text. Correspondingly, Ḥakham Faur writes that for the Greeks, "truth is *a-letheia* 'dis-covery' of a metaphysical reality lying 'out there'. The function of the Greek *logos* is...letting things be seen from themselves, passively."[22] Hence, reading is passive and meant to discover the intention of the author. Once that meaning is dis-covered (or perhaps un-covered) the text becomes useless.

As noted by J. R. R. Tolkien, author of *The Lord of the Rings,* his novel was not meant as an allegory for WWII. He specifically rejected allegory as "many confuse applicability with allegory, but one resides in the freedom of the reader, and the other in the purposed domination of the author."[23] The problem

---

22 *Ibid.*, p.17

23 J.R.R. Tolkien, *The Fellowship of the Ring,* (Harper Collins Publishers: New York 2012) p. xi. Tolkien was suggesting that authors dominate readers through allegory, which requires a particular interpretation of the allegory. In contrast, applicability allows the reader freedom to interpret and analyse the story. Interestingly, HaRaMBa"M, in the *Moreh,* recognises the Aggadot of the

with allegory, in Tolkien's view, is that it is used by the author to dominate the reader. In that case, the author is there telling the reader exactly how he is to understand the text. The job of the reader is to submit to the author's textual intention. By rejecting allegory, Tolkien was allowing the reader to approach the text intelligently and autonomously, based on the reader's specific circumstances.

Submissive reading is related to slogans/graffiti[24] and hieroglyphics. The slogan used to protest the Vietnam war, "make love not war," was readily understood by all: war is hateful and bad, while the obliteration of military force is loving and good. The meaning of this slogan was as clear to Americans living during the Vietnam war, as the meaning of a pictorial image of a bull was clear to Egyptians living in the days of the Pharaoh. Because hieroglyphics and graffiti leave no room for interpretation, they are well suited for submissive (or analphabetic) readers. Similarly, the chant, "let's go Brandon!" is clearly understood by contemporary USA residents, and it does not matter that there is no lexical relationship between the words "let's go Brandon," and the message being conveyed. That's exactly the point of graffiti and submissive reading: the author/speaker (and not the words/reader) decides for you what you are reading/hearing.

Let us conclude with a comment regarding that which lies at the core of Jewish alphabetic-consonantal thinking: the national written texts of Israel. The national written texts of Israel, also

Ḥakhamim as allegorical, and as requiring a different kind of reading than Halakha. Hence, in Aggada, the text is less important.

24 For a full discussion of the differences between graffiti and writing, see Jose Faur, *Golden Doves with Silver Dots* (Indiana University Press: Bloomington, 1986), pp. 1–17.

known as the written Torah, are those texts that were nationally published by the nation of Israel and formally placed in the Temple, in Jerusalem. Publishing these texts nationally positions them as the starting point and context for all discussions regarding wisdom, truth, law, ethics and even politics.[25] Jewish discussions start from and return to the national written texts of Israel because they are accepted by the nation as representing the wisdom of God. However, these texts are only the beginning of knowledge. Every individual, acting as a reader, must approach these texts independently, and use them to measure and evaluate the ever changing political and cultural landscape offered by the outside world. Because Jewish alphabetic thinkers had access to the written texts of Israel, they were rarely (if ever) mesmerised by demagogues peddling intellectually unimpressive ideas.

The Tyrant's Concern with Human Rights

The following dialogue takes place between Moses and the Pharaoh at the beginning of *Perashat Bo*. By way of background, at this point, Egypt had been decimated by seven plagues, the last of which destroyed much of the agricultural products of Egypt. Pharaoh's ministers (tellingly referred to as "the slaves of Pharaoh"[26]) are becoming impatient with the prospect of new plagues. They recommend to the Pharaoh that he just let the Israelites go "and worship the Lord their God, before you learn of the destruction of Egypt!"[27] It is important

[25] Jose Faur, *The Naked Crowd: The Jewish Alternative to Cunning Humanity* (Derusah Publishing: Ft. Lee, 2009), pp. 71–72

[26] Exodus 10:7

[27] *Ibid.*

to point out that there is one thing that terrifies tyrants, and petty politicians, throughout human history. This fear transcends national borders and is even transcultural: I refer to negative public opinion polls. Giving in to negative public opinion, Pharaoh finally grants Moses permission to go and worship God, inquiring "who exactly will be going"?[28] Moses informs Pharaoh that we will "be going with our young and elderly, with our sons and daughters, with our sheep and cattle, as for us, this is a celebration of God."[29] Pharaoh's reply is fantastic: "may the Lord be with you, if I send you and your children; behold that evil is before you... the men may go and worship the Lord."[30]

What Pharaoh is saying emphatically, if not lovingly [*sic*], is that he is the great protector of women and children, and that he for one, will not let them get harmed. Entering the desert wilderness is fraught with dangers (dehydration, sandstorms, snakes, etc.). How irresponsible of Moses to want to take women and children, in the name of religion (to worship God) away from the loving cradle of Egyptian civilisation and the protection of Tyrant Pharaoh. Pharaoh, the great defender of human rights won't let this happen. Listen carefully and you will hear the following words: "as the great benevolent leader that I am, it is my duty to protect the women and especially the children.[31] As the Pharaoh of Egypt, and in the interests of human rights and the protection of children, I will not let this happen! Only the men can go."

---

28 *Ibid.* vs. 8

29 *Ibid.* vs. 9

30 *Ibid.* vs. 10-11

31 Cf. the United Nations Committee on the Rights of the Child

As noted above, Tyrants recognise the power of dissolving the family. The men may go, while the women and children will stay in Egypt. Pharaoh would have fit in perfectly in the company of Charles Fourier and the other Marxists thinkers, since they all seek the dissolution of the family.

But there is another aspect of Pharaoh's strategy. It is the cynical use of fear and hysteria as a way to motivate the masses to do his bidding. This is a strategy used repeatedly by petty politicians and demagogues throughout history. Consider the following: was it not the Egyptian Pharaoh who decreed that all male babies should be thrown into the Nile River? Yes, it was. Therefore, we may ask: is the Pharaoh now looking to transform himself from a genocidal maniac who butchered untold number of newborn babies, to a protector of the children? No. He was not. Pharaoh's reply to Moses included the phrase, "behold, that evil is before you!"[32] Generating fear among the masses is a typical ploy used by Tyrants to manipulate these same masses into doing the Tyrant's will. Tyrants expertly and unabashedly stir mass fear and even psychosis among the populace, frantically pointing to looming threats, which are perceived by the people as real, but which are carefully selected by the Tyrant to promote a particular political or financial agenda.[33] In this case, Pharaoh attempts to use the fear of the dangerous desert as a way to manipulate Jewish mothers to protect their children from a reckless Moses. "The women and children must stay," is meant as a message to the Jewish mothers: "are you now going to recklessly endanger the

---

32 Exodus 10:10

33 In this context, it would be useful to do some additional research regarding "mass formation psychosis", and Dr. Robert Malone.

lives of your children and follow Moses into the dangerous desert?" The Jewish mothers, being expert readers, understood that the genocidal Pharaoh could not care less about the welfare of their children, and politely but resolutely rejected Pharaoh's offer to protect them.[34]

The wisdom of the Israelites was that they didn't fall for the con of the Pharaoh or of other tyrants. Hence, the story of Pesaḥ is the story of Jews, raised in *batim,* precisely reading the world around them, who say no to the protection of the Pharaoh, and who instead, seek out the word of God at Sinai.

> "For there is no one as free as one who toils in the study of the Torah."
>
> *Pirqe Abot 6:2*

✦

[34] In contrast, analphabetic people (Gentiles and Jews) unable or unwilling to think for themselves, heed the Tyrant's calls for panic and react often violently, as in the sadistic self-destructive deportation and execution of millions of farmers by Stalin and his mobs, which was necessary to rid the Soviet Union of evil capitalists. Cf. the Destruction of the Kulaks by Stalin in (*Wikipedia*, "Dekulakization"). Who needs God? Useful idiots certainly don't.

Maṣa or Crackers?

Rabbi Yitzhak Berdugo

Rabbi Yitzhak Berdugo was born and raised in South Florida. After studying at Yeshivat Beth Moshe Chaim (Talmudic University) in Miami Beach, Rabbi Berdugo received his bachelors in Talmudic law and *semikha* under the auspices of the *Rosh Yeshiva*, Rabbi Yochanan Moshe Zweig SHeLIṬ"A. While studying in New York, Rabbi Berdugo also received his *Yoreh Yoreh* from Rabbi Eliyahu Ben Haim, *Rosh Yeshiva* and *Av Bet Din* of BaDa"Ṣ Mekor Haim, Queens, NY, followed by a *Qabala* in *sheḥiṭa* and in lung checking. He has written much on Sephardi Halakha in addition to translating the works of great Sephardi *Rabbanim*. Currently residing in Miami Beach, Florida, Rabbi Berdugo serves as the *Rosh Kollel* of the Bal Harbour Kollel and is also studying for *Dayanut* qualification through the Eretz Hemdah Institute of Jerusalem and the Montefiore Endowment.

In recent years there has been a revival of the usage of soft *maṣa* for the *miṣva* on Seder Night. This trend has become exceptionally popular due to the convenience of being able to purchase commercially-made frozen soft *maṣa*. In this article, we will discuss the evolution of *maṣa* throughout the ages, the halachic ramifications, and the author's opinion of what is ideal for the *miṣva*.

Thick *Maṣot*

The Gemara brings a dispute between the schools of Shammai and Hillel:

> Bet Shammai states: One may not bake thick bread on Passover [as it might become leavened before it has a chance to bake]. But Bet Hillel permits it. [The Gemara asks:] And how much thickness is required for the *maṣa* to be considered thick bread? Rab Huna said: a *ṭefaḥ* [handbreadth thick], as we find that the shewbread was a *ṭefaḥ* [of unleavened bread]. Rab Yosef strongly objects to this: If the Sages said this by diligent [*kohanim* in the *Bet HaMiqdash*] would they say this with regard to [ordinary people] who are not as diligent? If they said this with regard to well-kneaded bread, would they say the same with regard to bread that is not well kneaded?
>
> *Pesaḥim 36b–37a*

As is usually the case, the Halakha follows the opinion of Bet Hillel and thus thick *maṣa* would be permitted. However, after Rab Yosef objected to Rab Huna's source for the limit of a *ṭefaḥ*, the Talmud did not define how thick *maṣa* can actually be according to Bet Hillel. As a result, we find different *shiurim* given by the *Rishonim*.

Meiri writes:

> One may not ideally bake very thick *maṣa* on Pesaḥ because a large part of the thickness will retain its moisture and inhibit [it from evaporating], causing the dough to become *ḥameṣ*. This thickness is a *ṭefaḥ,* however, anything under a *ṭefaḥ* would be ideally permissible.[1]
>
> *Meiri to Pesaḥim 36b*

This opinion is followed by Rabbenu Yeruḥam, *Ohr Zaruạ*, and *Ra'avyah.* Accordingly, once Rav Yosef raised his objections, only less than a *ṭefaḥ* would be acceptable.

In *Bet Yosef* Rabbi Yosef Qaro wonders why the Tur did not codify the maximum thickness of *maṣa*. R. Yoel Sirkis (*Ba"Ḥ*) explains that the *Tur* (as well as RI"F and RaMBa"M) did not codify the maximum size because although Rab Yosef objected to Rab Huna's proof from the shewbread, he did not actually object to the maximum thickness of a *ṭefaḥ*.

Interestingly enough, the *Shulḥan Ạrukh* does not follow the three pillars of the Halakha[2] and codifies the stricter opinion: "One should not make thick loaves that are a *ṭefaḥ* on Pesaḥ."[3] Nonetheless, anything up to a *ṭefaḥ* would be permissible.

However, we do find an even more stringent opinion. RITB"A (Rabbi Yom Tob Ishbili) cites his teacher Ra'a"H, who stated:

> Since [Rab Yosef] excluded the *ṭefaḥ* and the Gemara did not establish a permissible size, we may not make thick *maṣa* at all. And this is why it is the universal custom to make *reqiqin* [thin *maṣot*] for

---

1 *Meiri* to ibid.

2 RI"F, RaMBa"M, and Ro"Sh

3 *Shulḥan Ạrukh, Oraḥ Ḥayim* 460:5

the *mișva*. Nevertheless, after the fact up would be permissible as long as it is under a *țefaḥ*.

This opinion is followed by RaShB"A and *MaHaR"I Vayil* as well.

Sefer Abudarham and the *Kol Bo* cite RABa"D who stated an alternative reason for why *mașot* should be thin:

It is proper to make the *mașa* used for the *mișva* thin and small and not thick and large, as the latter is not considered *Leḥem Ọni* [bread of affliction].

ReM"A writes that *mașa* should be made as *reqiqin* and not thick like bread, for *reqiqin* are not as quick to leaven.[4] One may inaccurately (as is commonly done) interpret *reqiqin to refer* to the thin cracker-like *mașot* which are commonly used nowadays. Nevertheless, it is obvious that the *reqiqin mașot* used by the Rishonim were similar to the modern soft *mașot* that are eaten by Sephardic communities across the globe. *Kol Bo* states that the custom was to make three *mașot* from one *isaron,* which is equivalent to 3.4 pounds of flour (based on the calculations of R. Ḥayim Noeh). Accordingly, each *mașa* would weigh around 1.1 pounds, thus impossible to make unless it was soft. ReM"A himself actually quotes this custom.[5] Similarly, while RaMBa"M describes the procedures for the *Seder Pesaḥ*, he writes:

He takes two *reqiqin* [of *mașa*], divides one of them, places the broken half inside the whole and recites the blessing, *hamoși leḥem min ha'areș,*

---

4 *Oraḥ Ḥayim* 460:4

5 *siman* 475:7

which is obviously referring to soft *maṣa* by virtue of the fact that the broken half is placed "inside the whole."

Ḥameṣ Umaṣa 8:6

Even later Ashkenazi authorities such as R. Hillel Herz[6] state that the common custom was to bake thin *maṣot* with a thickness of a fingerbreadth. Certainly, *maṣa* that thick must have been soft, or else it would be nearly impossible to eat. Moreover, later Ashkenazi authorities such as *Ḥoq Ya'ạqob* and Seder *Eliyahu Rabba* cite Herz. Even *Mishnah Berurah* (486:3) and *Shulḥan Ạrukh haRav* (486:2) speak about spongy-like soft *maṣot* without expressing any reservations.

Seemingly it would clearly be permissible even for Ashkenazim to use soft *maṣa*. Consequently, Rabbi Hershel Schachter writes[7] that there is no custom that restricts Ashkenazim from eating soft *maṣa*.

However, Rav Asher Weiss writes[8] that although according to the letter of the law soft *maṣa* would be permissible for Ashkenazim, nevertheless there is a concern of *ḥimuṣ* since we are not experts in making them. Furthermore, he invokes the verse: "do not forsake the Torah of your mother."[9]

It is difficult to understand why "experts" would be required for baking soft *maṣa*, as it was done (mainly by housewives) throughout Jewish history. How could such an integral food which was made and eaten by every Jew require such levels of expertise? Furthermore, Rabbi David Ibn

---

6 *Bet Hillel*, 17th cent., Lithuania

7 *ketab yad* to R. Meir Rabi

8 *Haggada Minḥat Asher*, 5764, *siman* 15, page 322

9 Proverbs 1:8

Zimra[10] writes that there is no concern of *ḥimuṣ* since "our ovens are extremely hot and immediately stop any *ḥimuṣ* from occurring...especially with our *maṣot* which are extremely thin."

If early generations wrote that there is no concern when making thin, soft *maṣot*, why should we be concerned about the matter? Furthermore, any Ashkenazi who is not an expert can certainly purchase soft *maṣot* made by experienced bakers and thus avoid any concern. Alternatively, one who would like to bake their own *maṣot* could easily do a test run beforehand, to ensure that the recipe (and the directions being followed) sufficiently cook the inside.

It is also difficult to understand how one can legitimately invoke the verse from Proverbs — which inhibits innovation and deviances from customs — for as we mentioned above, the universal Ashkenazi custom for ages was, in fact, to use soft *maṣot*.

The *Berakha*

Maṣa is called *pat* (bread) and not *pat haba bekisnin* (certain types of snack foods for which the Gemara[11] requires an initial *Birkat Mezonot* and a terminal *Me'ẹn shalosh*). Furthermore, an essential part of the *Seder Pesaḥ* is the washing, *Hamoṣi,* and the *Birkat Hamazon.* However, *Shulḥan Ạrukh*[12] cites the opinion of Rab Hai Gaon, who states that any hard, cracker-like substance is considered *pat haba bekisnin*, not *pat*. If so,

---

10 I, 494

11 *Berakhot* 42a

12 168:7

one may ask — how can the common, hard *maṣa* suffice for the *miṣva* if it is not considered *pat* but rather a *mezonot* food?

This question has bothered many throughout the generations, and various attempts have been made to answer for and defend the custom of reciting *Hamoṣi* on hard *maṣot.*

Sephardic *Aḥaronim* such as Rab Ḥayim Pelagi, Rab Yosef David (known as *Bet David*), and Rab Moshe Zekhut dealt with this question, as apparently the *maṣot* used during their time were cracker-like. *Bet David* suggests that there is a difference between the process of making hard *maṣa* and crackers. He explains that *maṣot* are baked with the primary intent to cook the dough and only consequently turn hard due to the thinness of the dough. Contrarily, crackers are first baked and then returned to the ovens for intentional toasting. Therefore, *maṣot* would be *hamoṣi* since *maṣot* only become hard as a result of the natural baking process.

R. Samuel Florintin[13] suggests that in reality one should recite *Mezonot* on hard *maṣa*; however, due to the fact that there is no other option available during Pesaḥ, one recites *Hamoṣi.* Rab Abraham Alkalai[14] rejects Florintin's answer since it is simply possible to make thin, soft *maṣot.* He therefore sides with *Bet David.*

Nevertheless, it is hard to understand the *Bet David*'s novel distinction, since ultimately the final product tastes and looks like a cracker. Why should the intent determine the blessing when, in the eyes of the consumer, there is no difference?

13 *Ọlat Shemuel*, Saloniki, 17th cent.

14 *Ḥesed LeAbraham*, 19th cent.

The Development of Hard *Maṣa*

As noted above, even some Sephardic communities began using hard *maṣa*. The question is when and why?

R. Ya'ạqob ben Asher writes:

> I have seen that the meticulous ones in Barcelona bake everything they need for the holiday before the holiday so that if there was any mixture of *ḥameṣ* it would be nullified before it becomes *assur* [as only on Pesaḥ is *ḥameṣ* unable to become nullified].
>
> *Ṭur 448*

Evidently, as early as the 14th century in Spain there were already some "meticulous ones" who were baking everything before Pesaḥ. As a result, *maṣa* would be hard and thin since soft *maṣa* which is even half a fingerbreadth thick dries up within a day and becomes very difficult to eat. Thus, the *maṣot* baked would be extremely thin and cracker-like so that they would be able to last for the entire duration of *Pesaḥ*.

R. Ḥaim Benveniste (17th century) also mentions *Ṭur*'s ruling, stating that this practice was followed by some. It seems that the *minhag* of the "meticulous ones" spread until it became the universal custom in countries like Turkey. For upon tasting Yemenite soft *maṣa* in 1910, R'Yom Ṭob Ṣemaḥ testifies:

> How different are these *Maṣot* compared to the heavy indigestible flavorless [*maṣot*] that are made in Turkey. The *Maṣot* here in *Yemin (?)* are made twice daily with extreme care and without any concern of *ḥameṣ*.
>
> *Travels of Yom Ṭob Ṣemaḥ to Yemen*

R. Ya'aqob Sofer[15] documents that in Jerusalem (about 110 years ago), all Sephardim would bake their *maṣot* before *Pesaḥ*. He states that although some would use hard *maṣot* for the *Seder*, most would prepare *soft maṣot* on the eve of *Pesaḥ* specifically for the *Seder* (since it would stay fresh for the *Seder*) while the *maṣot* for the rest of *Pesaḥ* would be baked thin and cracker-like (for no other option was available). Similarly, R. Abraham Dangur (Iraq, 20th century) testifies that only the *maṣot* for the *Seder* were soft and around the thickness of half a fingerbreadth.

As people began relocating to urban cities, *maṣa* bakeries began to replace the traditional homemade *maṣa* and hard *maṣa* evolved to be the standard *maṣa* even for the first night of *Pesaḥ*. Even R. Abraham Bornsztain was pained that families stopped baking *maṣa* themselves:

> I have heard that it has become popular that households do not bake their own *maṣa* anymore but rather one person bakes and sells to others. This practice is very bad in my eyes. Why should one neglect such a precious *miṣva* and purchase *maṣot* from the market...Anyone who fears *Hashem* should follow the ways of his forefathers and bake *maṣot* themselves and be happy with the *miṣva* that comes to his hands.
>
> *Abnei Nezer 372*

Nevertheless, there were communities throughout the Middle East (usually in less developed cities) who would bake soft *maṣa* daily throughout *Pesaḥ* without concern of the stringency brought down by *Ṭur*.

---

15 460:44

Closing Thoughts

Although it is beyond the scope of this article, there are countless proofs throughout the words of *Ḥazal* which imply that the *maṣot* originally used were soft. However, due to a *ḥumra* that [ironically] developed in Spain, many communities began baking hard *maṣot* before *Pesaḥ* so that they would be preserved and edible throughout the entire *Pesaḥ*. This new type of *maṣa* created a dilemma since it seemingly no longer fits within the category of bread. So much so that R. Abraham Saba (15th century) writes[16] that one should not recite *Hamoṣi* or *Birkat Hamazon* on dried out *maṣa*.

Although the later *Aḥaronim* attempted to justify the blessing of *Hamoṣi* on hard *maṣa*, it is difficult to understand how one can recite "this is the bread of affliction that our ancestors ate in the land of Egypt," as they did not eat crackers. It is the author's humble opinion that even those who have the custom to be stringent (be they Ashkenazim or Sephardim), may (perhaps even should) eat soft *maṣa* nowadays thanks to the innovation of the freezer, as one can purchase *soft maṣa* made before *Pesaḥ*, which can stay fresh throughout the entire *Pesaḥ*, even if it was baked months before.

✦

16 *Ṣeror Ha'Mor*

Insights from the Future

By Selected Students of The Ḥabura

The Theological Battle of *Yeṣiat Miṣrayim*

Ben Rothstein

Ben Rothstein is a student at University College London studying Ancient Languages. He is originally from East Barnet and attended Yeshivat HaKotel for two years. He has been involved with youth activities for many years and currently works with his wife as a youth worker in the community.

The Talmud[1] observes a discrepancy between the way that the tenth plague, the death of the firstborn, is described in the Torah and the way in which it is related by Moses to Pharaoh. The Torah states that the plague took place "at exactly midnight" (בחצי הלילה),[2] whereas Moses describes the plague as occurring "at around midnight" (כחצת הלילה).[3] RaSH"I[4] quotes this question of the Talmud and brings its answer: Moses was deliberately vague in his description, lest Pharaoh's astrologers make a mistake with regard to the exact time the plague occurred and, consequently, declare Moses a liar. However, this in itself raises a question: would it really have made that much difference? For a pronouncement as fantastical and devastating to the Egyptians as the death of every firstborn in Egypt, would Pharaoh's astrologers truly not have believed that this was the same death of the firstborn predicted by Moses, simply because it appeared to be two minutes early?

A second question which arises from the story of the plagues concerns Pharaoh's unexpected response to Moshe during the plague of frogs. Pharaoh calls in Moshe and Aharon and requests that they entreat God to remove this second plague. However, when Moshe asks when to remove the frogs, Pharaoh instructs him the following day.[5] Why would Pharaoh wait for respite from the frogs? One would have expected his answer to have been an instruction that the frogs be removed immediately.

Thirdly, one of the motifs repeated throughout the narrative

1 *Berakhot* 4a
2 Exodus 12:29
3 *Ibid.* 11:4
4 *Ibid. s.v. kaḥaṣot halaila*
5 *Ibid.* 8:4-6

of the ten plagues is that of distinction. For example, "and I will distinguish on that day the land of Goshen upon which my people stand…and I will put a division between my people and your people,"[6] and similarly "and the Lord will distinguish between the cattle of Israel and the cattle of Egypt."[7] Although the principal result of the Exodus is the separation of the Jewish nation from the Egyptians, it is not clear why the text reiterates this point so insistently. A fourth question follows on from the previous point: After God declares that no cattle of Israel shall be felled by the pestilence afflicting the cattle of the Egyptians, Pharaoh sends out messengers to investigate if this is indeed the case.[8] What motivates Pharaoh to verify this claim? Moreover, why does the Torah deem it necessary for us to know that Pharaoh did so?

It would appear that Pharaoh is nonplussed by miracles *per se*; what matters are the details — the specificity and precision with which God, through Moshe, orchestrates and oversees the plagues. The reason for this is simple if we understand the mindset of Pharaoh and indeed the entire Egyptian nation. The theology of Ancient Egypt was that of polytheism; every power in nature had its own assigned deity, as well as different nations having their own gods, who frequently battled each other to prove who was the mightiest god of all. Against this cultural backdrop, Pharaoh's responses and actions become much more intelligible. The demonstration of a miracle is not in itself a novelty for a polytheist, who accepts the idea of deistic forces capable of (ostensibly) breaking the laws of nature. What God

6 Exodus 8:18-19

7 Exodus 9:4-7

8 *Ibid.* 9:7

is trying to prove to Pharaoh is not His existence, but rather His uniqueness, as expressed by His infallible omnipotence. The way to convince a polytheist of the truth of monotheism is to show absolute and complete control over all aspects of nature, down to the last detail. This attitude can in fact be inferred from Pharaoh's response to Moses and Aaron following their initial request to free the Jewish people: 'Who is the Lord, that I should hearken to His voice to send away Israel? I do not know the Lord, *and also* I will not send away Israel.'[9] Pharaoh's final statement consists of two parts, which can be understood as follows: (1) I have never heard of your God, (2) even if I had, I would still not obey Him and send Israel away. Thus, to Pharaoh, the existence of another deity, the God of the Hebrews, is nothing more than another entry to add to an ever-expanding pantheon.

The significance of the most minute details now becomes evident. Had the plague of the firstborn been even a little delayed, the Egyptians could have contended that another god was 'fighting' or disrupting God's attempts. Similarly, Pharaoh setting the time for the removal of the plague of frogs allowed him to truly test God's power, as the action must now be done on his terms. Ibn Ezra takes this specific point further and explicitly writes that Pharaoh thought that the alignment of the stars had caused the frogs to ascend from the Nile and that Moshe was using this to his advantage. Now that the time had come for the frogs to depart, Pharaoh requested that their departure be delayed in order to test Moshe's ability.[10] The distinction between Israel and Egypt mentioned in the fourth

---

9 *Ibid.* 5:2

10 Ibn Ezra, commentary to Exodus 8:6 s.v. *vayomer lemaḥar*

and fifth plagues serves to show that God can not only release wild beasts and a pestilence, but also control their movements once summoned. Hence Pharaoh's need to investigate whether or not there really did seem to be one God in total control, by seeing that no cattle of the Jews had been afflicted by the pestilence, and the importance of this to our narrative. Support for this interpretation can also be found in the fact that the *pesuqim* that discuss God's power to separate in the above instances are followed by the phrases, "in order that you will know that there is none like the Lord our God",[11] and "in order that you will know that I am the Lord in the midst of the land."[12] This implies that it is the distinctions and the precision, rather than the miracles themselves, that will prove God's uniqueness to the Egyptians.

To develop this theme a little further, many commentators suggest grouping the plagues into different categories. For example, the first three came from below the ground, either from the Nile or from the dust of the earth itself; the second three came about on the ground, affecting animals and humans directly; the third set of three all came from the sky. To the Egyptians, these would have been assigned to discrete powers, incapable of being governed by one supreme Being. God thus displays mastery over all regions of the physical world. Not only can God control these aspects, but He can also make a distinction between one area of land and another. God thus displays mastery over spatial physicality. Furthermore, He can control exactly when a plague will begin and end. God thus displays mastery over temporal physicality.

---

11 Exodus 8:6

12 *Ibid.* 8:18

More than simply displaying mastery over the physical realm with arbitrary plagues and miracles, from both modern research and statements of Ḥazal it is evident that there was deliberate intent within the content of the miracles, plagues, and commandments designed to disprove Egyptian theology. The *Midrash* states:

> At the time when the Holy One, blessed be He, told Moshe to slaughter the Pesaḥ, Moshe said to him: "Master of the world! How can I possibly do this thing? Do You not know that the sheep is the god of Egypt?"...The Holy One, blessed be He, said to him: "By your life! Israel shall not depart from here until they have slaughtered the god of Egypt before their eyes, that I may make known to them that their gods are nothing."
>
> *Shemot Rabbah 16:3*

The Midrash explicitly links the commandment of the Paschal lamb with an anti-polytheist agenda. Modern Egyptological research shows us that the Egyptian god in question is , *ẖnmw*, popularly Romanised as *Khnum* (alternatively an incarnation of Ra, see below), who was represented with the head of a ram (Figure 1). The Midrash goes on to link this idea with the *pasuq* "and I will mete out punishments to all the gods of Egypt,"[13] that against the gods of Egypt God will execute some kind of judgement, as if this were a "contest," so to speak. The *Zohar* identifies both the sheep and the Nile as part of the idolatry of Egypt and explains how the Pesaḥ offering was cooked in such a way as to be public and degrading.[14]

13 Exodus 12:12

14 *Zohar* II: 18a-b. One opinion there goes so far as to say that the entire purpose of the plagues was solely to disprove the theology of Egypt and not to punish the Egyptians whatsoever.

The ten plagues therefore were in fact targeted attacks against polytheism and whilst we will never appreciate the full extent to which the belief system of the Egyptians was uprooted, using what has been discovered about Ancient Egypt we can begin to build a bigger picture. To begin with, and developing Rabbi Yoḥanan's observation in the Zohar mentioned above, 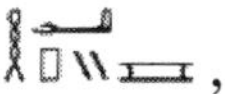, *ḥʿpy*, *Hapi* is the god of the flooding of the Nile,[15] from which Egypt derives its renowned fertile soil. The first plague, in which the Nile turned to blood, was a direct attack against this deity, inverting the source of life to become a symbol of death. Special mention ought to be made of the *pasuq* that recounts how the fish died and caused a repulsive smell to emanate from the Nile.[16] Fish had been venerated in Egypt from as early as the Old Kingdom (with possible predynastic influences), but in later dynasties also came to be regarded as taboo, especially for consumption.[17] This idea became so prevalent that the word *bwt*, meaning 'to detest' or 'an abomination',[18] was written with a fish determinative, as in

[15] It does not appear that the Egyptians considered the Nile itself to be a god; the word *ʾitrw*, meaning 'river,' never appears with a god determinative. Rather, it appears as if they deified the *flooding* of the Nile instead. The word for the flooding, *ḥʿpy*, can appear both with and without a god determinative, and although there are no discovered temples to *ḥʿpy*, there were nonetheless offerings to him. It is possible that the flooding was considered in some way associated with or originating in Osiris, see Mark Smith, *Following Osiris: Perspectives on the Osirian Afterlife from Four Millenia* (Oxford: Oxford University Press, 2017), 450.

[16] Exodus 7:21

[17] Douglas J. Brewer and Renée F. Friedman, *Fish and Fishing in Ancient Egypt*, The Natural History of Egypt II (Warminster: Aris & Phillips, 1989), 17-19

[18] Raymond O. Faulkner, *Concise Dictionary of Middle Egyptian* (Oxford: Griffith Institute, 1962), 82

.[19] Furthermore, despite the widely-attested existence of fish-offerings, "representations of fish-offerings to gods are highly exceptional";[20] the presence of the dead fish on the surface of the Nile confronted the Egyptians with an abominable and taboo sight. Additionally, the pungent miasma of dead fish was a familiar motif in Ancient Egypt and present in Egyptian literature. In *The Dispute between a Man and his Ba,*[21] a XIIth dynasty text, the man laments:

> Lo, my name reeks
> Lo, more than a catch of fish
> On fishing days of burning sky [i.e. a hot day].[22]

Moreover, once again the ancient words for bad smells utilised a fish determinative.[23]

In lower Egypt the iconography used in association with *Hapi* was that of the frog.[24] The frog itself is another example of an Egyptian deity (Figure 2), perhaps one of the oldest:

> The frog appears to have been worshipped in primitive times as the symbol of generation, birth and fertility in general; the Frog-

19 Alan Gardiner, *Egyptian Grammar: Being an Introduction to the Study of Hieroglyphs* (3rd rev. ed.) (Oxford: Griffith Institute, 1957), 476. Sign List K2.

20 Ingrid Gamer-Wallert, *Fische und Fischkulte im alten Ägypten*, Ägyptologische Abhandlungen XXI (Wiesbaden: Harrasowitz, 1970), 69, translation mine. Fish never appear on Offering Tables, with the exception of that of Amenemhat III, and this may have been intentionally shocking.

21 Papyrus Berlin 3024

22 Miriam Lichtheim, *Ancient Egyptian Literature, Volume 1: The Old and Middle* Kingdoms (Berkeley: University of California Press, 1973), 166

23 Gamer-Wallert, *Fische und Fischkulte*, 80

24 Richard H. Wilkinson, *The Complete Gods and Goddesses of Ancient Egypt* (London: Thames & Hudson, 2003), 106.

> goddess *Ḥeqet* or *Ḥeqtit*...was originally the female counterpart of *Khnum*...each of the four primeval gods, *Ḥeḥ*, *Kek*, *Nāu*, and *Amen* is depicted with the head of a frog... the cult of the frog is one of the oldest in Egypt, and the Frog-god and the Frog-goddess were believed to have played very prominent parts in the creation of the world.[25]

An innovative explanation of the fourth plague of *Ạrob,* based on RaSH"I, is proposed by Rabbi Dr Raphael Zarum. RaSH"I writes that the fourth plague was "all kinds of wicked wild animals and snakes and scorpions, in a mixture."[26] The Egyptian demoness , *ʿm-mwt*, *Ammit*, was believed to wait in the underworld to eat the hearts of those who were deemed impure and was depicted as a combination of a crocodile, a lion, and a hippopotamus (Figure 3), the three largest man-eating animals known to the ancient Egyptians. Rabbi Zarum suggests that the "mixture" to which RaSH"I refers is in fact one animal formed of a mixture of wild animals, and that in the fourth plague, "God brought [*Ammit*] to life."[27] Another more obvious example is , *rʿ*, *Ra*, the sun-god. The plague of darkness obscured one of the most powerful symbols of the Egyptian pantheon. *Ra* was believed to have ruled over all three realms; that is, the sky, the earth and the underworld,[28] paralleling the arrangement of the sets of threes of the plagues. Additionally, *Ra* in the underworld is also depicted as having a ram's head (Figure 4), recalling again the imagery of the Paschal lamb.

25 E.A. Wallis Budge, *The Gods of the Egyptians: Or, Studies in Egyptian Mythology*, II (1904), 378

26 RaSH"I, commentary to Exodus 8:17 s.v. *et he'ạrob*

27 LSJS, "Exodus and Egyptology: Tips for the Seder"

28 George Hart, *A Dictionary of Egyptian gods and goddesses* (London: Routledge & Kegan Paul, 1986), 179

Of course, the above list is not exhaustive, and there are many aspects of ancient Egyptian culture still unbeknown to us. However, the point is clear:

> Th[is] contest was far more than dramatic humiliation of the unrepentant and infatuated tyrant. It was nothing less than a judgement on the gods of Egypt. The plagues fell on the principal divinities that were worshipped since times immemorial in the Nile Valley… we see that we have here a contrast between the God of Israel, the Lord of the Universe, and the senseless idols of a senile civilisation.[29]

God used specific imagery and iconography in His punishing of the Egyptians to uproot and destroy the polytheistic theology that existed among the Ancient Egyptians, and had likely been absorbed to varying degrees by the enslaved Israelites as well, demonstrating for all to see that He alone is God.

Epilogue: The Significance of the Knowledge of YHWH

In all the *pesuqim* mentioned previously, God is consistently referred to by the Tetragrammaton (for convenience, henceforth written as YHWH). I would like to briefly delve deeper into the significance of this name and thereby reveal the way in which this is particularly pertinent to the Exodus.

The opening *pesuqim* of *Parashat Va'era* are obscure, referring to God by both YHWH and other titles:

> And *Elohim* spoke to Moses, and said to him 'I am YHWH. And I appeared to Abraham, to Isaac and to Jacob as *El Shaddai*, but my name YHWH I did not make known to them.
>
> *Exodus 6:2-3*

[29] J.H. Hertz, *Pentateuch & Haftorahs* 2nd ed. (London: Soncino Press, 1978), 400.

Not only are the meanings of these names as yet unclear, but ostensibly the above statement is incorrect; God does indeed appear to Abraham with the divine name YHWH. However, upon further scrutiny of the *pasuq* in question, a further oddity is revealed.

The *pasuq* states:

> And He said to him, "I am YHWH, who brought you out from Ur of the Chaldees to give to you this land, to inherit it." And [Abraham] said, "*Adonai Elohim*,[30] how will I know that I will inherit it?"
>
> *Genesis 15:7-8*

God introduces himself as YHWH, and Abraham replies with the words "*Adonai Elohim*." What did God try to communicate to Abraham and what message did Abraham receive?

According to the RaMBa"M, the only true name of God is that of YHWH; the other 'names' are instead epithets used to refer to God, but they do not capture any of His essence. He states explicitly that the uniqueness of the name YHWH is that it "expresses a clear expression of [God's] essence, that has no partner,"[31] i.e. that it cannot be used in reference to anything besides God. All other epithets used for God, including *Elohim*, can be used to describe other beings, and are in fact used in polytheistic contexts to refer to false gods. For example, the head of the Canaanite pantheon is *El*, from which *Elohim* is derived.

---

30 Although the consonantal text reads the Tetragrammaton, the Masoretic tradition vocalises this as *Elohim*.

31 *Moreh Nebukhim* I, 61

Perhaps one could suggest that God is telling Moshe that, until now, there has not been a true, overt demonstration of YHWH in the world. Even Abraham, who came to know God on his own, could not fully comprehend what Moshe, with His unique level of prophecy, could: that God is something totally apart from, incompatible with, and omnipotent over this world.[32]

Relating this back into the story of the Exodus, we see now why the understanding that God is YHWH is crucial to the theological message. The idea of God as *Elohim* was not unpalatable to Pharaoh; in fact, this expression of God was already known to him, as the *pasuq* recounts "and Pharaoh said to his servants, 'Could we find another like this one? A man in whom is the spirit of *Elohim*.'"[33] The concept of God that Pharaoh is unaware of is that of YHWH. At first, as discussed above, he is prepared to acknowledge the existence of another deity. However, the statement God intends to make through the ten plagues and the Exodus is to show something of His true essence, as expressed by the name YHWH; that is, of a single, omnipotent God, whose name and essence cannot be coupled with anything.[34] In summation, the content of the plagues was calculated and deliberate, intended to show the

---

32 A similar but not identical argument is made in *Nefesh Haḥayim*, III, 13:2, with overt Qabbalistic themes.

33 Genesis 41:38. Although whether this Pharaoh is the same as the Pharaoh of the beginning of the enslavement is subject to dispute (see *Ẹrubin* 53a), this *pasuq* still indicates that a deity known as '*Elohim*' was known to the Egyptians.

34 See also *Zohar* I, 195a, which makes this observation and comments that it was this specific point, the theology of monotheism, that Pharaoh found impossible to accept.

Egyptian theology as false, and direct the minds of both the Egyptians and the Israelites towards an appreciation of the monotheism of YHWH.

✦

Figures

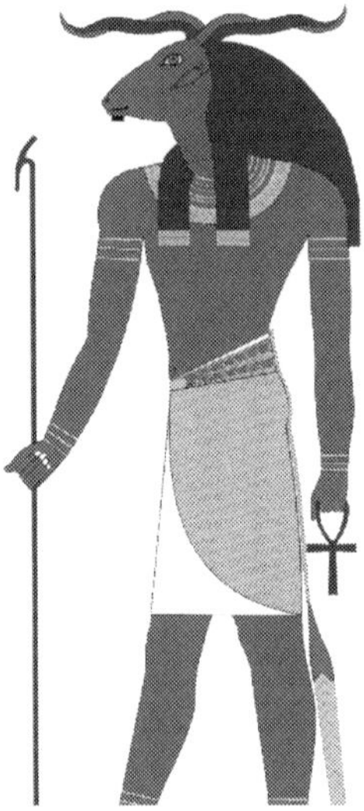

Figure 1: Khnum

Figure 2: Heqet

Figure 3: Ammit

Figure 4: Ra in the Underworld with the Head of a Ram

The Educational Methods of Moshe Rabbenu

Rabbi Jack Cohen

Rabbi Jack Cohen is the Associate Rabbi at Hampstead Synagogue, in London. He studied in Yeshivat Har Etzion and received *semikha* from both Rabbi Rimon (Mizrachi) and Rabbi Zalman Nechemia Goldberg *a"h*. He has a degree in philosophy from UCL and currently lives in London with his wife and two sons.

The end of *Parashat Bo*[1] brings the enslavement of the People of Israel to an end as they walk out of Egypt a free people. In its characteristically concise style, the Torah documents the actual Exodus in a mere sixteen verses, leaving fifty-four to describe a set of ritual practices that the People must observe. In revealing these new laws, we read of the manner in which they are transmitted from God to Moses, and also how Moses subsequently transmits them to the People. Our focus in this essay will be on how the Torah presents the differences between the words of God and the words of Moses, and what this teaches us about Moses' prophetic role.[2]

We start with a minor discrepancy. God describes to Moshe the rite of the Paschal Offering to be performed on the night proceeding the Exodus:

> Speak to all the congregation of Israel, saying…And they shall take the blood, and put it on the two side posts and on the upper door post of the houses, in which they shall eat it.
>
> *Exodus 12:1-7*

However, when Moses reports this to the People, we see a significant addition:

> And take a bunch of hyssop, and dip it in the blood that is in the basin, and touch with it the lintel and the two side posts, with the blood that is in the basin; and none of you shall go out at the door of his house until the morning.
>
> *Exodus 12:22*

---

1 Exodus 12-13:16 (All Biblical translations follow the *Koren* edition.)

2 We will focus on additions not *omissions* in this regard. The additions are certainly more interesting as the omissions are likely a product of the Torah's succinctness.

Whilst the fundamental law has not changed, Moses has introduced hyssop and a basin into the equation.[3] Here Moses does not just transmit the Law but takes it upon himself to give practical guidance on how to carry it out — specifically, by collecting the blood in a basin, and then using a plant as a brush to daub it onto the relevant parts of the door.[4]

To pre-empt any potential concern at this stage, we must note that it is indeed possible that all of Moses' words are simply a repetition of what God told him. It is possible, after all, that the hyssop passage was an element that was received directly from God and that the Torah did not feel the need to document that fact. Whether this is true or not is not our concern — our focus here is on how the Torah chooses to *present* events to us, and it chooses to present Moses innovating practical advice not received from God to help the People fulfil the new commandment. Furthermore, even if we are reading words that Moses stated of his own accord we need not be alarmed. Whilst RaMBa"M famously writes that each and every word of the Torah was dictated by God to Moses, it is perfectly plausible that God told Moses to include words that he had previously spoken of his own accord.[5] Indeed, much of the book of Deuteronomy seems to be Moses' own content and not his bare repetition of God's Word — nonetheless God instructed him to include it in the Torah.

---

3 There is a minor change in that the order of *mezuzot* and *mashqof* is reversed but this is not our focus here.

4 See Ibn Ezra to Exodus 12:7, *s.v. Ạl Shtei HaMezuzot.*

5 See the eighth of HaRaMBa"M's Thirteen Principles of Faith.

Returning to our original discussion, we now focus on the commandment of the annual Paschal Sacrifice which the People must perform. God tells Moses:

> And this day shall be to you for a memorial; and you shall keep it a feast to the Lord; throughout your generations shall you keep it a feast by ordinance forever.
>
> *Exodus 12:14*

When Moses relays it to the people much is added:

> Then Moses called for all the elders of Israel, and said to them, draw out and take you lambs according to your families, and kill the Pascal Sacrifice. And you shall observe this thing for an ordinance to thee and to thy sons forever. And it shall come to pass, when you shall come to the land which the Lord will give you, according as he has promised, that you shall keep this service. And it shall come to pass, when your children shall say to you, 'what mean you by this service?' That you shall say, it is the sacrifice of the Lord's Passover, who passed over the houses of the children of Israel in Egypt, when he smote Egypt, and delivered our houses.[6]
>
> *Exodus 12:21-26*

First, Moses tells the People that this rite is to be enacted once they enter the Land, although this is not a particularly novel introduction, considering at this stage (prior to the sin of the Spies) the plan was for the People to be in the Land the following year. Far more striking however is the insertion of an educational element into the mix. Moshe observes that there is an educational opportunity which will inevitably arise from performing this commandment and tells the People that it is an opportunity to recount the events of the night preceding the

6 Exodus 12:21-26

Exodus and pass the memory of that event on to the next generation.[7] Here, Moshe is not necessarily stating that this is the *only* Divinely intended purpose of the commandment, but nevertheless it does provide a rationale which the People can easily understand and which encourages their commitment to be meaningfully observant.

A similar format is found regarding another law — the sanctification of the firstborn. God tells Moses:

> And the Lord spoke to Moses, saying: Sanctify to me all the firstborn, whatever opens the womb among the children of Israel, both of man and of beast: it is mine.
>
> *Exodus 13:1-2*

Moses transmits this Command to the People as follows:

> thou shalt set apart to the Lord all that opens the womb, and every firstling that comes of a beast which thou hast; the males shall be the Lord's...And it shall be when thy son asks thee in time to come, saying, What is this? that thou shalt say to him, By strength of hand the Lord brought us out of Egypt, from the house of bondage: and it came to pass, when the Pharaoh would hardly let us go, that the Lord slew all the firstborn in the land of Egypt, both the firstborn of man, and the firstborn of beast: therefore I sacrifice to the Lord all that opens the womb, being males; but all the firstborn of my children I redeem.
>
> *Exodus 13:11-15*

---

7 By the Mishnaic period, telling the story of the Exodus in response to children's questions prompted by unusual rituals already followed a clear formula (*Mishnah, Pesaḥim* 10). The origins of this practice, which we have come to know as the *Haggada*, is directly drawn from Moses' additions as found in the verses here, as well as the others that we are about to see. Indeed, the very word *Haggada* is drawn from Exodus 13:8 — "*VeHigadeta.*"

Moses is not only stating the commandment here, but is also presenting its rationale, developing its details, and discussing the resultant future educational opportunities generated by the commandment.

Moses' helpful and insightful additions are rational and logical inferences based on an understanding of the commandments in their full context. It is perfectly reasonable to assume that the sanctification of the firstborn is tied in with the plague of the firstborn suffered by the Egyptians. Likewise, it is reasonable to assume that the repetition of a sacrificial ritual performed at an important historical juncture will play a role in the preservation of national memory.

By incorporating these explanations into his transmission of the Law, Moses is functioning as a uniquely effective intermediary who understands both the word of God and the mind of the People, and who is able to fully articulate the one in terms of the other. Nowhere is this process more apparent than in the relaying of the commandment for *maṣot.* God says to Moses:

> Seven days shall you eat unleavened bread; but on the first day you shall have put away leaven out of your houses: for whoever eats leavened bread from the first day until the seventh day, that soul shall be cut off from Israel. And on the first day there shall be a holy gathering, and on the seventh day there shall be a holy gathering to you...And you shall observe the commandment of unleavened bread; for on this very day have I brought your hosts out of the land of Egypt: therefore shall you observe this day in your generations by an ordinance forever.[8]
>
> *Exodus 12:15-17*

8 Exodus 12:15-17. (Here, unlike in the previous two cases, God gives Moshe the commandment *and* the reason— "for on this very day...")

The commandment itself is presented to Moses immediately following the rules of the generational Paschal Offering. Indeed, it is logical to combine the transmission of these two commandments, both binding future generations, both arising from and linking back to the Exodus. Nevertheless, there is a major problem with the presentation of this commandment. The purpose of the commandment of *maṣa* and proscription of leaven is to recall the Exodus. It recalls the Exodus because the People of Israel ate *maṣa* and not leaven when they left because their dough did not have time to rise:

> And Egypt was urgent upon the people, that they might send them out of the land in haste; for they said, We are all dead men...And the people took their dough before it was leavened, their kneading troughs being bound up in their clothes upon their shoulders...And they baked unleavened cakes of the dough which they brought out of Egypt, for it was not leavened; because they were driven out of Egypt, and could not delay, neither had they prepared for themselves any provision.
>
> *Exodus 12:33-39*

As can be ascertained by the verse numbers, the commandment regarding *maṣa* was given to Moses *before* the People of Israel had left Egypt and experienced their dough not rising. At this stage the commandment would mean nothing to the People.[9] Moshe addresses this problem in a simple yet brilliant manner. Prior to the Exodus he relays God's laws about the Paschal Offering to be performed in Egypt,[10] which was, of course, time

---

9 It is true that they had previously been commanded to eat *maṣa* with the Paschal Sacrifice (Exodus 12:8) but this would only take on its full meaning after the events of the Exodus.

10 Exodus 12:21-23

sensitive information. He immediately follows this by informing them that they will repeat this rite annually.[11] Teaching all the laws pertaining to the Paschal Sacrifice in one go obviously makes a lot of sense. Next, Moses withholds the commandment of *maṣa* until after the Exodus. At the time of the Exodus, haste had prevented their dough from rising and the People had thus been compelled to eat *maṣa*. After the Exodus, twenty-seven verses later, when the People had the appropriate contextual awareness required for their full appreciation of the Law, Moses finally informed them:

> And it shall be when the Lord shall bring thee into the...which he swore to thy fathers to give thee...that thou shalt keep this service in this month. Seven days thou shalt eat unleavened bread, and on the seventh day there shall be a feast to the Lord. Unleavened bread shall be eaten for seven days; and there shall no leavened bread be seen with thee, neither shall leaven be seen with thee in all thy borders. And thou shalt relate to thy son on that day, saying, this is done because of that which the Lord did to me when I came out of Egypt.[12]
>
> *Exodus 13:5-8*

Again, we see the introduction of an educational element — "*and thou shalt relate to thy son*" — at a time when it would indeed make sense to them given their experiences.[13]

---

11 Exodus 12:24-27

12 Exodus 13:5-8

13 If correct, then this implies that the People of Israel did not know of the prohibition to eat bread and the obligation to consume *maṣa* at the time of the Exodus itself. Indeed, this seems to be in accordance with the plain understanding of the verses in these chapters (see Ibn Ezra and Samuel David Luzzatto to Exodus 12:39). However, the Mishna (*Pesaḥim* 9:5), as explained by the Gemara (96a-b) states that there was an obligation to observe the commandment to eat *maṣa* and

To summarise: In the section of the Torah which we have analysed, we saw that Moses' role extended far beyond simply transmitting the Law of God to the People of Israel. Whilst the laws were faithfully conveyed, Moses also furnished the People with relevant practical advice (the hyssop), provided rationale for the Laws (the generational Pesach Offering, the sanctification of the firstborn), and was careful to choose the best time to teach the laws too (as seen with *maṣa* and leaven). In short, Moses' role was not just to teach the Law but to convey it in a manner which made it accessible and agreeable to the People of Israel. Moses aimed to help the People not just know the laws but be able to connect to them too — to show them their goodness and wisdom. In this manner he helped the People see that the laws were there to benefit them.[14] This is something that Moses would go on to tell the people explicitly: "keep the commandments of the Lord, and his statutes, which I command thee this day for thy good."[15]

All Torah leaders and educators ought to learn from Moses' example. Their role is not just to teach Torah, but to provide their students with context and explanations which emphasise

---

refrain from leaven on the day of the Exodus and the night proceeding it (see RaMBa"M's explanation of the Mishna). This has led several commentators (such as RaMBa"N) to argue that the Torah actually documents this observance (RaMBa"N and Ḥizquni to Exodus 12:39). Still, the source for the Mishna's homiletical reading of the verses is based on juxtaposition and not on their plain sense. It can therefore be argued that the Mishna is reflecting on the fact that the People of Israel did technically observe the eating of *maṣa* by consuming it with the Paschal Sacrifice, and did technically refrain from leaven since their dough did not rise, and as such technically observed the commandments around *maṣa* for one day, despite the fact that they received no formal command to do so.

14 This sentiment is doubtless the motivation behind RaMBa"M's statement in *Mishneh Torah* (*Temura* 4:14).

15 Deuteronomy 10:13

its vitality and relevance. Individuals who have not benefitted from such instruction should take on the responsibility to educate themselves in this manner.[16] If we diligently pursue this goal then we can realise in our own lives, and in the lives of those around us, the deeply personal connection to the Torah and its laws of which our liturgy so eloquently speaks — that they are "our lives and the length of our days."

✦

16 *Ibid.* See also *Mishneh Torah* (*Talmud Torah* 1:4.)

Reflections on Superstition at the *Seder*

Michoel Chalk

Michoel Chalk is originally from London and began his yeshiva study at Kerem BeYavne in 2016. Having completed the IDF Hesder programme there, he resides in Israel pursuing a degree in Cognitive Sciences at the Open University while working as a security bodyguard.

The first night of Passover is arguably the evening most central to the Jewish year. The Torah advances it, and the ceremonies surrounding it, as the primary setting within which to present our tradition, faith, and gratitude to succeeding generations. Through a large variety of factors, in tandem with its incredible significance to our nation — maybe precisely because of it — the *Seder* has become a highly ritualised event. Sometimes it has even been presented as a theatrical performance, in settings as diverse as children's Pesaḥ plays and the Christian Eucharist. This provides a perfect setting for ritual to solidify into superstition.[1] In this essay I will use the term "superstition" in its most general sense and not specifically in relation to the Halakha.

The Catechism of the Roman Catholic Church has provided a succinct definition, attributing:

> an importance in some way magical to certain practices otherwise lawful or necessary. To attribute the efficacy of prayers...to their mere external performance, apart from the interior dispositions that they demand, is to fall into this superstition.[2]

Many sages throughout the ages have espoused this kind of "superstitious" approach, but others have been just as vociferous in putting forward the "rationalist" alternative which will be the focus of this piece.[3] If we are not to take the superstitious approach, there is little significance in the *qelipa*, or outer shell,

1 Ritual is characterised by J. Z. Smith as 'a mode of paying attention.' See *To Take Place* (1987), p. 103.
2 Catechism 2111
3 A brief outline of both approaches may be found in Rabbi Dr. Nathan Slifkin's book, *Rationalism Vs. Mysticism.*

of a given rite. It is incumbent on us to infuse it with meaning. *Seder* Night is central to our childhood experience, and the lessons we learn through it have long-lasting repercussions. We must seriously evaluate the material we present, and its basis, because it is a foundation of tomorrow's Judaism.

What follows are three illustrations from the *Haggada* of ambiguous customs which have been appropriated for the purposes of both approaches. For each one, after briefly tracing its development, we will see something of how it fits into a broader picture, or what it might mean for us. The second part of this essay will discuss the popular song *Ḥad Gadya* (both its history and the various approaches to its interpretation), followed by a conclusion suggesting a broader perspective on its significance.

The first incursion of superstition into the *Seder* meal may be identified at the point where we recite the *He Laḥma Ạnya* text.[4] With this text we begin our celebration of the night by transporting ourselves back to Egypt: The *maṣot* in front of us are reminiscent of those our ancestors ate in slavery. Although we cannot partake of the Paschal lamb, next year may God grant that we do so. Thus runs the text.

A question posed by many commentators is why we begin in Aramaic when most of the *Seder* is in Hebrew. Curiously, different manuscripts of the *Maḥzor Viṭry*[5] offer strikingly different interpretations. The Moscow manuscript states simply that the use of Aramaic was "because this was their language" in

---

4 Originally written entirely in Aramaic (see, for example, *Seder Rab Saadia Gaon*), some Hebrew words have crept back into versions appearing in most modern rites.

5 a version of the prayer book modelled on the practices of *RaSH"I* (1040-1105)

Babylonia where this introductory text was presumably instituted.[6] Indeed, many early sources recommend translating both *He Laḥma Anya* and the *Ma Nishtana* into the vernacular for the benefit of less educated participants.[7] An older version of the book, the Sasson manuscript, offers a more sinister view: In *Pesaḥim* 109b, Rab Naḥman expresses the view that on *Seder* Night we are protected from demonic harm, yet it is necessary that we should take extra precautions. He posits that our invitation at the start of the meal is in Aramaic so that demons, who only speak Hebrew, will not understand and "gate-crash" to ruin the festivities.[8] Rabbi Moshe Cordovero (1522-1570) is even more demon-cautious, stating that demons indeed *can* understand Aramaic. He reminds us that earlier in the day we will have burned all *ḥameṣ* in our possession, symbolically ridding ourselves of our sins and thus the forces of evil. As a conciliatory gesture we therefore open our *Seder* in Aramaic, an impure tongue, thereby inviting Satan back (to some extent) into our homes.[9]

These varied explanations within the very opening of the *Seder* demonstrate how our world perspectives are likely to

---

6 This resonates with *Ta'anit*, from whence it seems that not all of this formula was unique to the Seder rite. The text, which continues "next year in Israel," was after all clearly not composed there. If so, the invitation to "*Pesaḥ*" most likely refers to partaking in the Passover festivities, not specifically the Paschal lamb. This could resolve a problem raised by Rabbenu Tam, cited in *HaManhig*.

7 Rabbi Yiṣḥaq ibn Ghiyat in the name of Rab Naṭronai Gaon (re. *Ma Nishtana)*, *Maḥzor Viṭry*, *HaManhig*, *Orḥot Ḥayim*.

8 Although both approaches are reiterated by several early commentators, this one is most likely the original version of *Mahzor Viṭry*. This manuscript is older, and the answer also matches that given by RaSH"I elsewhere, in *Sefer HaPardes*.

9 *Siddur* of ReMa"Q, quoted in *Ṭaạmei HaMinhagim*. This type of concern for Satan is not a new idea in some Jewish mystical circles – see, for example, chapter 45 of *Pirqé deRabi Elięzer*.

influence the way we interpret a text. Through the concept of *Torah Shebe'ạl Peh* (Jewish oral law), we are granted the power of interpretation – the ability to see the text's relevance to our own day.[10] Nonetheless, it would be irresponsible to present our own personal interpretation as though it were a text's sole and originally-intended meaning, without being aware of the effect that our cultural mindset has on us. *Torah Shebe'ạl Peh* is a powerful gift, yet "with great power comes great responsibility."

In the *Maggid* section of the *Haggada*, we arrive at the passages detailing the plagues. As we do so, starting from "blood, fire and plumes of smoke" through the specific ten plagues in Egypt and their tripartite abbreviation, we mark each plague by spilling wine from the cup. Many explanations are offered for this ritual practice, ranging from it being an expression of sympathy with the Egyptians[11] to the more vengeful idea of removing the plagues from ourselves (in contradistinction to Exodus 15:26) to transfer them to our persecutors.[12] Whereas the first interpretation (espoused by Rabbi S.R. Hirsch and many other influential commentators) is nowadays the more popular, the second has not entirely died out. A notable Rabbi from Baltimore reports his practice of a custom (of Iraqi origin) of pouring this wine on a neighbour's

---

10 This conception is derived from *Antiquities of the Jews* 13:193, *Mishnah Makot* 1:10, *Leviticus Rabbah* 32:8, *Baba Meṣiạ* 59b, *Menaḥot* 29b, *Temura* 16a, and the outline of R. Elijah of Vilna's approach found in the introduction to *Pe'at HaShulḥan*, amongst other sources. See also the discussion in Joshua Berman's *Ani Maamin* (2020) on common vs. statutory law (p. 138).

11 Commentary of Abarbanel to the *Haggada*.

12 MaHaRI"L, citing Rabbi Shalom of Neustadt

doorstep in order to bring down a curse on their home.[13] (We are informed that he was not on good terms with this neighbour. He reports that the first year he tried this their dog died, the next year their house burnt, the third year the husband died. At this point he stopped, his vengeful spirit presumably satisfied.) As such, this is a prime example of superstition in ritual.

It goes still further: In many oriental communities (most commonly Moroccan), this wine, associated with divine retribution, is feared. It may not be looked at, and certainly not drunk by the children. Rabbi Joseph Dweck has pointed out how this is antithetical to the nature of the evening.[14] The *Seder* is a setting in which we strive to absorb and impart conviction in God's mercy, justice, and special covenant with us. By maintaining practices whereby we attempt to seize control of God's reins and steer the universe — not through His ways but by spilling wine, we deny all three.[15]

This brings us to another area in which demons may have made their way into the *Haggada* — here, wine does not generate the problem; rather, it thwarts it. Although we famously drink four obligatory cups of wine at the Seder, there is a mysterious fifth cup, accredited in some manuscripts to the Talmud itself.[16] It is poured mainly amongst Ashkenazic communities and consumed only in some Yemenite

13 For similar customs and their explanations see Rabbi Professor David Golinkin's article from 6th April 2016 at *Schechter.ac.il.*

14 in a class delivered to The Ḥabura, publicly available on YouTube

15 This attack is applicable not to the basic custom itself, but rather to one of the possible intentions with which it may be fulfilled. Fulfilling it with other intentions in mind can indeed be deeply edifying.

16 See *Pesaḥim* 118a and RI"F (1013-1103) to there.

communities. HaRaMBa"M (1138-1204), following the Geonim, recommends its pouring and drinking as optional. It is commonly referred to as "the Cup of Elijah the Prophet." What is its meaning?

Rabbi Shem Tob Gaguine (1884-1953) connects this to another practice (first evidenced, to my knowledge, in the 1453 Ulm-Treviso illustrated *Haggada*) of opening the door to welcome Elijah. According to *Rosh HaShana* 11b, the *Seder* Night has retained its relevance as a "night of anticipation"[17] even through modern times, for it is at this time that we can expect the final redemption. Hence, in the last part of the Seder, when we move from reminiscing on the past to praying for the future, Ashkenazim open the door to be ready to greet Elijah, the herald of redemption,[18] even pouring him a cup of wine, in the event that he might choose to stay and dine.

On the other hand, R. Yuspa Shammes of Worms (1604-1678) [19] states that Elijah's cup refers to a custom of uttering his name to ward off demons.[20] Rabbi Isaac Baer Levinsohn (1788-1860)[21] notes that according to Rab Naḥman in the Talmud, the four Passover cups are grouped together and therefore could make their drinker susceptible to magical (though not demonic) attack.[22] Thus the solution, for those who wished, was to add a

---

17 Exodus 12:42

18 Malachi 3:23

19 Cited by Leor Jacobi, "The Fifth Passover Cup and Magical Pairs"

20 Attracted by the fourth cup, c.f. the discussion in *Pesaḥim* 109b. C.f. Rabbi Moshe Isserles' glosses and *ḤaTa"M Sofer* to *Shulḥan Ąrukh, Oraḥ Ḥayim* 480.

21 *EFe"S Damim*, conversation three (this part of the piece is omitted in *Keter Shem Ṭob*)

22 This is one possible understanding of Levinsohn, though probably not the most accurate. Inconsistencies such as those pointed out by Me'iri *ad locum* could provide another explanation. Most simply, Levinsohn might see the "fifth cup

fifth cup, restoring the total to a more propitious number.[23] Leor Jacobi suggests that in time, as the superstition became less popular, the original reason for the additional fifth cup was lost.[24] Thus this practice, too, may have had its roots in superstitious beliefs, but here, as opposed to seeing the *superstitionalisation of a ritual* (as defined above: "a mode of paying attention"), we seem to see the *ritualisation of a superstition.* An action to safeguard against sorcery became a poignant pointer to God's future redemption.

Another interesting perspective may be gained through the lens of *Seder* songs. Whereas hymns are part of every festive meal, on Passover they appear to take on a special significance. From a historical perspective, *Nirṣa*[25] was not so much a stage of the Seder as it was a footnote; as late as 1813 a French *Haggada*'s *Nirṣa* section is composed of the single narrator's line: "If he completed each section as ordered, it will find favour: May it be favourable before God, thus may be [His] will, Amen."[26]

On the other hand, Gershom Scholem recalls an experience shared by many — that in his assimilated family, "...everyone read the hymns at the end [of the *Haggada*], albeit a very distorted version. The tunes were more

approach" as Amoraic in origin (thus pseudepigraphic) and conflicting with the opinions of Rab Naḥman and the other *Amora'im* there.

23 In some, but not all, Amoraic circles, even-numbers were thought to strengthen evil forces. See *Pesaḥim* 110b.

24 "The Fifth Passover Cup and Magical Pairs"

25 The last stage of the Seder according to the most widespread mnemonic, dating back to 12th century France. Commonly including various songs or hymns, it can be literally translated as "It has found favour."

26 *The Bordeaux Haggada*, housed in the Moldovan Family Collection, republished through Nahar-Stavit in 1987

popular and memorable than the words."[27]

In most printed versions of the modern *Haggada*, *Nirṣa* includes songs of praise relating the events of the night, as a kind of extension of the *Hallel*, followed by two cumulative but seemingly unrelated songs, *Eḥad Mi Yodeyạ* and *Ḥad Gadya*. The latter two first appear in print at the end of the Prague 1590 edition of the *Haggada*, but their roots extend much further back. The less-controversial one is probably *Ḥad Gadya*, and on it we shall now focus.

The Song's History

Although the narrative style and the accumulative/recursive format of the story narrated in *Ḥad Gadya* are more ancient still, the oldest extant manuscript of the text (in any language) is found, as far as I know, in a 13th century French *siddur*,[28] written in a Sephardi hand completely in Aramaic.[29] This *siddur* contains the prayers for the entire year and concludes with its version of

---

27 1974 interview with Muky Tsur, *Debarim BeGo* 1982

28 As opposed to the modern version which is interspersed with Hebrew. The relevant page can be viewed online at the Bibliothèque nationale de France's *Gallica*, "Prières juives pour toute l'année (France)," folio 140v.

I was alerted to this version's existence, as well as that of *Qibuṣ Mạberot* referenced later on, at The Hebrew University of Jerusalem's Jewish Music Research Center, "Had Gadya in Israeli Culture."

29 The *Haggada* commentary of Rabbi Yedidya Tia Weil mentions a manuscript from the Synagogue in Worms, but says nothing about its date. That of Rabbi Elieẓer Swardschorf quotes the head of the Serock Bet Din (presumably the historian and scholar Rabbi Yosef Levinstein), who points out that the line '*Ḥad gadya dizvan* (unique but accurate spelling) *aba bitrei zuzei* (defective spelling) *ḥad gadya*' has the same numerical value as the Hebrew for 'I am Yehonatan Ben HaỤzi'el.' This appears to be the only reference in any literature to Yonatan ben Ụzi'el by that spelling.

the *Haggada*. At the end of this *Haggada*, seamlessly following on from the *Hallel*, is a dirge comparing the very first Passover festivities, celebrated as the Exodus from Egypt was taking place, to the dire situations in which Jews were subsequently forced to celebrate Passover. This leads into a hymnal exegesis of Canticles 2:10 as God's call to leave the baseness of Egypt for the beauty of Israel. Following that is a page of what appears to be handwriting practice, and only then, on the last page with content, we find *Ḥad Gadya*. It is thus unclear whether it was meant to be associated with the *Haggada* or was simply placed in its vicinity by chance.[30] Certainly, there is nothing in its content to indicate any connection to the *Seder*, or even to Judaism in general. Additionally, whereas the version common nowadays is explicitly religious in nature — ending with God putting an end to the emissary of death — this version is not. It will suffice to quote the last verse as a demonstration:

> (Then came the cat and ate the rat
> that gnawed the rope
> that harnessed) the ox
> that drank the water
> that slaked the fire

[30] Another manuscript (*MSS F45166* at the National Library of Israel), the *Sereni Haggada*, dated by Sivan Gottlieb (*"Go and Learn": The Ashkenazi and Italian Roots of the Sereni Haggada*) to the end of the 15th century, contains *Ḥad Gadya* on the last page, after all of the hymns, after instructions for the counting of the *Omer*, and even after the concluding word, '*saliq*'. Like the earlier Provençal version, it is in full Aramaic, written in a later hand than the rest of the manuscript, and includes a mouse (although in a seemingly nonsensical position, indicating garblement of an earlier tradition). This time, however, like the printed version, it continues the chain all the way to God, places the cat towards the beginning and also includes a Yiddish translation.

that burned the rod
that beat the dog
that ate the goat
that father bought for two *zuz*; one goat.[31]

The origins of the modern version, and how it became attached to the *Haggada*, are thus shrouded in mystery. Such literature has close parallels in folk and children's songs around the world, but this appears to remain the earliest version recorded.[32]

The first appearance of the version of *Ḥad Gadya* widespread today is in the 1590 Prague edition of the *Haggada*, accompanied by a Yiddish translation. As noted, it closely resembles songs for children from other cultures, though it may be that those songs were themselves influenced by *Ḥad Gadya*. It is possible that it was sung by children (or even adults) on *Seder* Night to keep them awake — a certain mental alacrity is required to perform a fast and flawless recitation of the lengthy but easy verses.[33] This

---

31 The initial part of this text (enclosed by parentheses here) is found in a later script (14th-15th Sephardi Provençal). According to Dr. Ẹzra Chwat, it is unclear whether the copy of the rest of the song in an earlier hand predates it (personal communication).

32 See Newell, "The Passover Song of the Kid and an Equivalent from New England," *The Journal of American Folklore*, Jan. - Mar., 1905, pp. 33-48. Also: See *ibid.*, p. 45 for a less-similar example from *The Panchatantra*, not mentioning a goat. It may be no coincidence that in Sanskrit a *gadya* is a statement or story told in prose. Taking the serendipity one step further: this word is itself derived from *GaDa* (to speak clearly), sharing a stem with the Hebrew *HaGaDa*.

33 Indeed, in the *Sereni Haggada*, the final pages (before the subsequrntly-added *Ḥad Gadya*) contain illustrations of a hunting scene including a dog seizing in its mouth the leg of what must be a cat as it is poised to pounce on a bird. It is unclear if the illustrator was familiar with the *Seder* ceremonies (Sivan Gottlieb, ibid.), but this could point to an oral tradition of singing a song along the lines of *Ḥad Gadya* at the end of the *Seder*. Rabbi Isaac Baer Levinsohn in *EFe"S Damim* (ibid.) speaks of an old German or Yiddish "almanac" containing children's songs and games,

would be in keeping with other customs such as "snatching [the] *maṣot*," which the Talmud itself recommends to help children stay alert.[34]

Explanations of the Song's meaning

Already in 1699, not too long after the first print publication of the song, Johann Christof Wagenseils, a Bavarian Hebraist, was searching for its meaning.[35] He asked Jews from Italy, France, Holland, and Germany, but none of them could offer him any clues. In desperation, he turned to Christian Knorr von Rosenroth, a fellow Christian and an eminent student of the Qabbala, but he claimed that this science could shed no light on the subject. In later travels, Wagenseils visited Prague itself, the scene of the first printing of the song. A Jewish Qabbalist he met there asked for some time to consider the issue, and added that if no meaning were known, one could surely still be discovered. Sure enough, he then sent in a letter the first exegesis of *Ḥad Gadya*, the details of which are as follows: There

including a version of *Ḥad Gadya* exactly as we have it but ending with the butcher. If this is true, all other discussion on the point is moot, however it is unclear whether he actually saw such a work or if he was simply speculating on its existence.

34 *Pesaḥim* 109a. One proponent of this view is Rabbi Isaac Baer Levinsohn, who notes that at Roman banquets, after which the *Seder* is modelled, riddles were also passed around (*EFe"S Damim, ibid.*). Another, R. Shem Tob Gaguine, notes that 'even among enlightened nations are found such songs' (*Keter Shem Ṭob,* ed. 1942, III, p.214).

35 Much of the following paragraph is summarised from Wagenseil, *Belehrung der Jüdisch-Deutschen Red-und Schreibart* (1699), and from Hermann von der Hardt, *In Bigam Superiorem, De Minerva Graecorum, and Et Haedo Judaeorum*, (1727). I owe thanks to Yoni Goldstein of Baltimore for helping me with accurate German translations from the former.

are to be two Messianic figures who will usher in an age of eternal justice and atone all sin; one of them, *Mashiaḥ ben Yosef*, will be sacrificed in the process. Several times he tried making his appearance, but each time his purpose was defeated by the shortcomings of the generation. *Ḥad Gadya* symbolically details these various travails and transmigrations of the messianic figure.

In fact, this exegesis seemed so Christological in its underlying assumptions, (a messiah, son of Joseph, required *ab initio* to atone sin, through his death) that in 1727 another scholar, Provost Hermanno Von der Hardt, came to the conclusion that the Jews knew the secret of the song all along — the time required to respond was needed only to devise a suitable explanation that would cover the real story by appealing to Christian sensitivities. The real, hidden explanation, he said, was a history of the Jewish people as reflected by the Land of Israel. In brief, his explanation suggested that the last verse of the song is actually a description of the process which we will summarise here as follows: The Messiah will take back the land from the Turks, who wrested it from the Christians, who conquered it from the Saracens, who took control after the fall of the Romans, who followed the Greeks, who conquered it from the Persians,[36] from the Babylonians, from the Assyrians, from the Israelites whom God redeemed through Moses and Aaron, thus restoring it to Jewish dominion. Von der Hardt claimed that this last nationalistic twist was precisely what the Jews were hiding.

To compare, we can examine the following interpretation:

36 For comparison, in Wagenseils' Prague Qabbalist's reading, the Persians are the last stage before God, thus leaving contemporary nations out of the picture.

Composed some years later, it is the first known interpretation of the song by a Jew, for Jews — that of Rabbi Elijah, *Gaon* of Vilna. Summarising again with the final all-inclusive paragraph, we have: Then came the Holy One, blessed be He, and destroyed the Angel of Death, who killed *Mashiaḥ ben Yosef*, who destroyed Edom,[37,38] which conquered the Jewish assembly, which had rebuilt the Temple,[39] which had defeated the merit of the staff of Moses, which struck Pharoah,[40] who had punished the jealousy of the sons of Jacob, who had afflicted Jacob, who had acquired the birthright for bread and lentil brew; one goat to Esau (the blessing, to appease him), and one goat to Jacob (the birthright).

Common to each of these explanations is the opinion that the song outlines a historical progression, giving special significance to each symbol along the way. Besides the fact that we have seen that this is not the original sequence order, a problem (already noted by Von Rosenroth) is that it is difficult to imagine a set of criteria that would include so many details of Jewish history, yet omit so many others.

RaMBa"M teaches that even a parable containing a message can have extraneous details,[41] a principle which has been applied by many contemporary commentators to this song. Their interpretations are somewhat less stiff than the ones so far described, and they often look at the general pattern, not the details. A communal settlement in Israel, Qibuṣ Mạberot, has published one such interpretation. Their Modern Hebrew

37 i.e. the empire which began with Rome

38 Some versions read "baseless hatred."

39 Alternatively: "subdued the Evil Inclination"

40 Alternatively: "the Egyptians"

41 end of introduction to section I of *Moreh Nebukhim*

rendition of the classic piece ends with God's declaration that this has "gone too far" and His subsequent decision "to start all again from square one, this time with no mistakes."[42] They present the cycle of violence in the song as indicative of a broken world in which the smallest flaw, or *pegam*, is perpetuated by reactionary participants until it reaches cosmic proportions. In the end, it is this cosmic fragmentation itself which is the factor necessitating the direct Divine intervention that will herald a new age of perfection. This is perceived from the pattern of ever-increasing magnitude, but not from the details. Using the same method, Chava Alberstein concludes her song with the remarks:

> Tonight I have another question,
> When will end this apprehension,
> The pursuer is pursued, the smiter struck,
> When will this vicious spiral stop?
>
> *Chava Alberstein, Ḥad Gadya*[43]

Although the modern version of the song gives closure by having God as the final dealer, until this actually happens, for Chava, her fifth question goes unanswered.

Finally, in examining *Ḥad Gadya*, Franz Rosenzweig looks not at the details of the song, nor even at its structure, but rather at its place in the Seder, and at the Seder's place and role in the calendar, equipping the younger generation with the tools they require to become leaders themselves. His focus is the structural evolution which develops during the *Seder* amongst the

[42] This is a stylistic, rather than exact, translation.
[43] This is a stylistic, rather than exact, translation.

participants from autocracy to democracy:

> The father of the family speaks, the household listens, and only in the further course of the evening is there more and more common independence until, in the songs of praise and the table songs of the second part of the meal, songs which float between divine mystery and the jesting mood begot by wine, the last shred of autocracy in the order of the meal dissolves into community.[44]

When discussing all this with a friend of mine he asked me, "So who's right?" Obviously if we try to understand the original intent of the author of the song, most of these explanations have no hope of being "right"; they don't even have the right lyrics. On the other hand, if we try to understand what each one meant when they sang it, it would be difficult for them to be wrong. In either case, however, I believe that Franz Rosenzweig is correct. When first sung, it may have been an independent venture to assist a French child struggling to stave off sleep. When Rabbi Elijah of Vilna sang it, it was about a return through exile to the blessing of the firstborn. In either case, the tools are being given over and a double legacy of responsibility and leadership is being passed from one generation to the next. In the words of Natan Alterman:

> It was a spring day…
> When the father and goat entered the *Haggada*…
> It was already full from so many Miracles and wonders enormous in magnitude.
> So they stood on the last page, huddled together against the wall.
> The book smiled and said…
> Blood and smoke march through my pages…

44 Glatzer, *Franz Rosenzweig: His Life and Thought* (1961), p. 320

> But I know that a sea is not split for nothing,
> and that there is a reason to penetrate walls and wilderness,
> as long as at the end of the story,
> stand a father and goat,
> awaiting their turn to shine…[45]

We have seen that although practices — or the outer shells of our rituals — often stay the same, their souls, what they mean to us, never stagnate. Within the framework of God's immutable kindness to us, the more minor points are tailored by each generation to impart beliefs which are important to it. As is the case in the *Yaḥaṣ* section of the *Haggada*, the best is saved for later. The children always continue to ask their questions, and there will always be more answers to explore.

✦

[45] *HaGedi Min HaHagada, Dabar* newspaper, 7 April 1944, p. 2

The Manna Episode: Principles for Providence[1]

Sina Kahen

Sina Kahen was born in Iran and moved to England at the age of 3. He works in the Medical Technology and AI industries and is the author of *Ideas* (a series of books on the weekly Torah portion). He studied Biomedical Sciences, has an MBA from Imperial College, and lives in London with his wife Talya and two children. Sina is also the Co-Founder of The Ḥabura.

---

[1] Much of this essay is based on *Sermon XVI* of Rabbi Benjamin Artom's *Book of Sermons.* I have attempted to maintain the core message of that wonderful essay, while expanding on it with my own understanding of the manna episode and what it can teach us.

Throughout human history, our species have utilised communication in order to achieve connection. Words help us connect with one another, and humans seek connection naturally. A common form of communication is complaining.

The art of complaining has been part of human life for millennia, with the earliest known record of a complaint dating back to c. 1750 BC Babylon.[1] Prior to that and since then, humans have tended to search for reasons to complain! After all, the human brain is geared for survival, so it needs to focus on negatives (which appear more threatening to survival) more so than on positives (less vital for survival). Our brains perceive negatives at an approximated ratio of 5:1, so there seems to be more to complain than to be grateful for.[2] In many ways, complaining signals the complainer's need for attention and connection.

This psychological baggage from evolutionary development can even influence many to look around at their circumstances and challenge the Providence *(hashgaḥa)*, and even the Existence, of God. They question the possibility that a Creator would ignore His creation's complaints, leading to a denial of Providence. As the Psalmist states[3], "The fool said in his heart there is no God."

This evolutionary tendency to complain as a bid for

---

1 The complaint tablet to Ea-nasir is a clay tablet that was sent to ancient Ur, written c. 1750 BC. It is a complaint to a merchant named Ea-nasir from a customer named Nanni. Written in Akkadian cuneiform, it is considered to be the oldest known written complaint. It is currently kept in the British Museum, London.

2 William Berry, "The Psychology of Complaining," *Psychology Today*

3 Psalms 53:2

connection was prevalent among our ancestors too, especially after they left Egypt:

> "In the wilderness, all of the Children of Israel complained to Moses and Aaron."
>
> *Exodus 16:2*

> [Previously], they complained about water. Now, they complained about a lack of bread and meat because they had already consumed most of their cattle, for thirty days had passed since they left Egypt.
>
> *Abraham ibn Ezra, Commentary on the Torah*

> "The people were looking to complain."
>
> *Leviticus 11:1*

> As the people entered the desert, they experienced a variety of uncomfortable sensations. These complaints were very displeasing in the ears of the Lord, seeing they were caused by the fact that instead of marching joyfully towards their destiny and the Holy Land, the people marched only grudgingly.
>
> *Baḥya Ibn Paquda, Commentary on the Torah*

Among the many Providential elements of the Pesaḥ narrative, there is none more sublime than the provision of manna, "the bread of Heaven."[4] Ironically, this wonder occurred directly after Israel's complaint:

> If only we had died by the hand of the Lord in the land of Egypt, when we sat by the fleshpots, when we ate our fill of bread! For you

---

4 Psalms 105:40

> have brought us out into this wilderness to starve this whole congregation to death.
>
> *Exodus 16:13*

> Advance toward the Lord, for he has heard your complaining.
>
> *Exodus 16:9*

To begin to appreciate the meaning behind this astonishing episode of our people's journey to physical and mental emancipation, we must explore the context and content of the manna story to see if there are principles to be uncovered.

The Background

When our ancestors left the shackles of Egypt behind them, they were nevertheless deeply imbued with the superstitious and ignorant ideas of that land. Their Egyptian masters practiced and promulgated the most unfortunate corruption of the human mind — idolatry.

> Under the rigours of an oppressive subjugation like that of Egypt, it was natural to expect retrogression. Slavery always demoralises man, cramps his intellect, debases his sentiments, and checks the aspirations of his soul.
>
> *Rabbi Abraham Pereira Mendes, Book of Sermons, IX*

To purge themselves of such thoughts and habits, Israel required much change and, as it were, a total re-wiring, both physically and mentally. To undergo the mental change that is required to 'know God,'[5] Israel would soon be given food for the psyche –

[5] See *Moreh Nebukhim*, I, chapter 34. Although one can never know the essence of God, one can still know Him through His ways and expressions (*derakhim*) such as His Word (Torah) and His world. Similarly, one can never know the essence

the Ten Commandments. However, before this challenge could be undertaken, God granted them food for the body – manna.

God acted as does a loving mother toward her son, when before letting him undertake a great mental work, she provides for the satisfaction of his material wants, so that, by the strength of his body he may be prepared for the exertions of his mind.[6] Just before this manna is to appear for the first time, God speaks to Moses:

> And the Lord said to Moses, "I will rain down bread for you from the sky, and the people shall go out and gather each day that day's portion — *that I may therefore test them, to see whether they will follow My instructions or not.*"
>
> *Exodus 16:4*

The following questions naturally arise after reading the last sentence of this profound verse: In what way does this Heavenly food constitute a proof of Israel's commitment to God? What exactly is God testing?

As we explore this manna episode further, I propose the following answer: God is ready to grant what we reasonably demand, but we must never expect God to exercise His Providence without our own involvement. *Berit* – like all meaningful relationships – requires responsibility and action from both partners.

Therefore, as we recite the *pesuqim* dedicated to the manna episode, we can start to sense certain principles of Providence, and these include (1) labour, (2) moderation, (3) faithfulness, and

---

of another person, but can 'know' that person through their expressions, persona, and works.

6 Rabbi Benjamin Artom, *Book of Sermons*, XVI

(4) gratitude. As we discover and expand on each principle, we can enhance our understanding of what was required of our ancestors then, and what is required of us today.

Labour

As the early morning dew lay on the ground, the manna appeared for the first time. The people were exhorted to "go out and gather."[7] Rather than command the appointment of officers to collect for the community and avoid potential confusion, God demands that Israel go out and gather the manna themselves. What a lesson! This great law of labour was therefore proclaimed to all future generations, teaching us that Providence will not allow those whom it protects to be idle:

> Wise people never remain idle; they fill their life with useful tasks, with virtuous actions; they consider labour as the friend of man, as the first of his duties, as his consoler when gloomy thoughts haunt his mind.
>
> *Rabbi Benjamin Artom, Book of Sermons, XVI*

> Man has not been created to sit idle with his hands folded in his lap.
>
> *Rabbi Yiṣḥaq Moshe Arama, Aqedat Yiṣḥaq, 55:1:6*

When the Psalmist states[8] that "you shall enjoy the fruit of your labours," it is reminding us that God assists us if we assist ourselves – God gives us bread if we labour for it!

To broaden this primal principle, we come to learn that the manna was to be made available only "early in the morning."[9]

---

7 Exodus 16:14
8 Psalms 128:2
9 Exodus 16:21

If this early opportunity was missed, "the sun was hot, and the manna melted."[10] This reality ensured that laborious activity begins when the day begins, with no time for extended slumber.

> Morning sleep is a cause of man's death.
>
> *Pirqe Abot 3:10*

> The rule is that one should engage his body and exert himself in a sweat-producing task each morning.
>
> *RaMBa"M, Mishneh Torah, Hilkhot De'ọt 4:3*

Moderation

Moderation is the second condition which Providence imposes. This second observation can be deduced from what Moses proceeds to say to Israel, on behalf of God:

> This is what the Lord has commanded: "Gather as much of it as each of you requires to eat, an *ọmer* for every man."
>
> *Exodus 16:16*

Therefore, the Providence of God demands that man should avail himself, according to his needs and wants, with moderation.[11] As we can all appreciate, this is not as simple as it seems. The ever-increasing accessibility to abundance has led to the increasing hubris of Western man, yet the laws of Israel are careful to curb such insatiable desire:

> A person should never eat unless he is hungry, nor drink unless thirsty…One should not eat until his stomach is full.
>
> *RaMBa"M, Mishneh Torah, Hilkhot De'ọt 4:2*

---

10 *Ibid.*

11 Moderation or 'the golden mean' is expressed in a variety of forms in both Biblical and Rabbinic works, including Proverbs 4:27, Ecclesiastes 7;16, *Ḥullin* 58b, and throughout *Hilkhot De'ọt*.

It is easy to imagine just how charmed our recently enslaved ancestors would have been by the palatable taste of the manna, and how tempted they would be to accumulate great quantities of it. This is why they were commanded to only take that which was their mandated portion, and not more. As our sages tell us: "Who is rich? He who rejoices in his portion."[12] Epictetus concurs when he states that, "He who does not grieve for the things which he has not, but rejoices for those which he has, is a wise man."[13]

Faithfulness[14]

After gathering their entitled portion of *manna*, our ancestors are ordered not to "leave any of it over until the morning."[15] As Abraham ibn Ezra clarifies, they were not to keep *leftovers* of the manna to eat on the next morning. Rather, they were to go and

---

12 *Pirqe Abot* 4:3

13 Epictetus, *The Encheiridion*, no. 129

14 There is much misunderstanding today concerning the term *emuna*. The root of the word *emuna* lies in Biblical and Rabbinic literature, where it connotes "faithfulness," "trust," "reliance," and "acceptance." Later philosophers use this terminology with additional meanings. Due to the lack of technical philosophical terms in Hebrew, *emuna* was first used in rendering the Arabic term *itiqad,* used by RaMBa"M (See *Moreh Nebukhim* 1:50), which refers to reason-based belief. The word *emuna* continued to be used in this original sense in the Jewish philosophical literature through the 13th and 14th centuries as many scientific works were transmitted to the west and translated from Arabic to Hebrew. Later, as scholasticism began to influence Jewish thought, *emuna* took on the meaning of "faith" in the sense of blind acceptance, authority-based assent, or *fides*. For an analysis, see Charles H. Manekin, *Hebrew Philosophy in the Fourteenth and Fifteenth Centuries: an Overview*, p. 353. For an example of the term *emuna* used by Ḥazal in its original connotations of "faithfulness" and "trust", see *Shabbat* 31a. For an example of the term *emuna* used in Scripture, see Exodus 17:12, Psalms 92:23, Isaiah 33:16, and Jeremiah 15:18, among others.

15 Exodus 16:19

gather their portion that falls from Heaven each day. The people "paid no attention"[16] to this order, and many proceeded to keep such leftovers. This led to the manna becoming "infested with maggots" and "stinking." The irony! What was received as a wondrous sign from Heaven above was suddenly exposed to the normal decay of physicality on earth.

The Talmud addresses this matter as it questions why God chose to provide the manna each day, rather than provide it all at once:

> The students of R. Shimon ben Yoḥai asked him: "Why didn't the manna fall for Israel just once a year to take care of all their needs, instead of coming down every day?" He said to them: "I will give you a parable: To what does this matter compare? To a king of flesh and blood who has only one son. He granted him an allowance for food once a year and the son greeted his father only once a year, when it was time for him to receive his allowance. So, he arose and granted him his food every day, and his son visited him every day."
>
> *Yoma 76a*

By not keeping leftovers, Israel would "focus their hearts to their Father in Heaven,"[17] and show their faithfulness *(emuna)*[18] in God, by trusting that the manna would descend on the following day. The only other outcome would be relentless hoarding driven by a mistaken perception that the gift of manna was no more than a fluke. Such faithlessness destroyed their food, and such faithlessness would ultimately destroy Jerusalem in the future.[19]

---

16 Exodus 16:20

17 *Yoma* 76a

18 See above footnote concerning *emuna*.

19 *Shabbat* 119b: "Jerusalem was destroyed only because there were no trustworthy people left there."

Gratitude

As much as labour, moderation, and faithfulness are prerequisites to its reception, Providence cannot persist upon a thankless heart. Rumi beseeches us to "wear gratitude like a cloak," and Cicero reminds us that "gratitude is not only the greatest of virtues, but the parent of all others."[20] Our own cherished sages incorporated gratitude in our daily worship when they enjoined us to declare: "We give thanks to You, that You are the Lord our God, and God of our ancestors, forever and ever."[21]

In the manna episode, the Children of Israel are to demonstrate their gratitude by devoting one day in the week to cease work, as the manna was not to be found on the Sabbath: "Six days you shall gather [manna]; on the seventh day, there will be none."[22]

Although this command was eventually abided by, it was initially ignored by some of our stiff-necked ancestors: "Yet some of the people went out on the seventh day to gather…but they found nothing."[23]

Just as our ancestors found no manna when gathering on the Sabbath in their day, we find no blessing from labouring on the Sabbath in our day:

> Alas! Even today, many Israelites who can gather plenty of manna during the week, whose labour and speculations are so fruitful, are not satisfied and will go out on the Shabbat to gather. They deny

---

20 Cicero, M. TVLLI Ciceronis Pro Cn. *Plancio Oratio*, 80

21 *Modim* blessing of the *Amida*: מוֹדִים אֲנַחְנוּ לָךְ שָׁאַתָּה הוּא ה׳ אֱלֹהֵינוּ וֵאלֹהֵי אֲבוֹתֵינוּ לְעוֹלָם וָעֶד.

22 Exodus 16:26

23 Exodus 16:27

> Providence that small token of gratitude. They set a bad example to their brethren, and call upon themselves the contempt of other nations by their scandalous disobedience to the law of Sinai.
>
> *Rabbi Benjamin Artom, Book of Sermons, XVI*

> Engaging in creative work on the Sabbath tramples the entire Covenant. It completely dissociates oneself from the concept of partnership and the endeavour in creating and developing our very own existence and everything around us, as partners with God. If one is not concerned with that partnership, then the Sabbath does not matter. But if one is concerned with that partnership, then the Sabbath is everything. And everything rests on guarding it.
>
> *Rabbi Joseph Dweck*[24]

Conclusion

In the Torah's description of the manna episode, we have been able to discover and explore four conditions by which our people can secure the blessings of God's Providence. The outcome of our efforts in garnering such Providence by opposing a happenstance, lazy, or distant attitude to God and His world is clearly undeniable. After all that our People have been through in history, what were the odds that we would survive? That our identity would persist? That our wisdom would be shared? That the topic of this very book would garner interest?

It is our labour, moderation, faithfulness, and gratitude to God's Word and world that have secured us such Providence. Every year, the manna can serve as a reminder for us all to fulfil these four conditions imposed by God's Providence, so that we

---

24 *Shabbat: God's Bond with Israel,* lecture at the London School of Jewish Studies (5779)

can accept God's invitation to enjoy our own version of Heavenly bread in our own times...

Come, eat my bread...that I have formed.

Proverbs 9:5

✦

The Memory of *Ạm Yisra'el*

Mijal Cohen Medresh

Mijal Medresh was raised in a family that transmitted a deep love for Torah and Arts. She studied at Midreshet Lindenbaum and Midreshet Rachel V'Chaya and has continued to study Torah ever since. She graduated from film school and has specialised in the areas of screenwriting, directing and editing. Mijal currently lives in Mexico City with her husband Albert Cohen.

> In each and every generation a person must view himself as though he personally left Egypt, as it is stated: 'And you shall tell your son on that day, saying: It is because of this which the Lord did for me when I came forth out of Egypt.'
>
> *Mishna Pesaḥim 10:5*

What is *Am Yisra'el*'s relationship to the past? Does the concept of History exist for the Jewish people? Does Israel understand its past experiences in a manner that differs from the way other nations experience theirs? In this essay, I will try to examine an idea of Ḥakham José Faur concerning the "National Memory" of the Jewish people and extrapolate it with regard to our experience of the *Seder* Night of Pesaḥ.

As mentioned by Ḥakham Faur and other Ḥakhamim, in Hebrew there is no equivalent to the word "History": the concept that alludes to the past is referred to as *zikaron*, which means something completely different. While history aims to objectively portray what happened in the past, *zikaron* implies involvement, a subjective and meaningful process that will lead to future action.

> One [history] has to do with the past, the other [memory] with the future...In Hebrew, the word for 'remember' (זכור) comes from the root (זכר) 'male'. It has to do with 'fertilization' and 'generation,' rather than retrieving an experience. When Scripture urges to 'remember (זכור) the Sabbath,'...it is not instructing us to 'recollect' but to transform belief in Creation into a day of rest...Thus, when the liturgy proclaims that the Sabbath is 'a reminiscence (זכר) of the acts of Creation' it is referring to a generative process, the outcome of such a belief — not the 'remembrance of things past.'
>
> *Jose Faur, The Horizontal Society, p. 215*

Historical method is an attempt to discover by research what actually happened in the past, but it often fails to do so. All reported events involving human beings are coloured by subjectivity, ambivalence, and cultural narratives. Even when two people agree on the facts, they will rarely agree on their meaning. Therefore, the past is a territory to which we have no access, other than that which is gained by our being heirs to a reliably transmitted memory.

The Torah, when speaking of the past, operates under the terms *zikaron* and *morashah*, where *morashah* denotes National Memory (thus indicating both identity and transmission). Scripture is not a book that only contains cold facts; it is not a history textbook. The Torah is the national book of *Ạm Yisra'el*, from which we have drawn through the generations; values, laws, culture, teachings, stories, and an identity. It is worth mentioning that each word of the Torah is true and was dictated by God to Moses. However, as the Torah has a narrative format in which it selects information and highlights certain details, people, or events, its perspective is singularly and specifically that of *Ạm Yisra'el* itself.

> National Memory is what people wish to transmit to their posterity...National memory involves commitment to an ideal envisioned by your ancestors that you accept and wish to pass on to your children. It has to do with your ethos and national culture and matters transcending 'factual truth' and 'cold facts'.
>
> *Jose Faur, The Horizontal Society, p. 215*

The event of the past that is most evoked in the Torah and in the daily life of a Jew is *Yeṣiat Miṣraim,* "so that you may remember the day of your departure from the land of Egypt as long as you live."[1] The Exodus constitutes the most important event in the memory of *Ạm Yisra'el*. Just as on a personal level, memory is necessary to forge an identity, the same thing happens on a national level. Our identity as a nation is born from the collective consciousness that we acquired as a people at the Exodus from Egypt and especially in its climax during *Matan Torah*, in which personally, as well as collectively, we intensely and closely experienced the existence of God, divine intervention, the delivery of His Law, and the eternal covenant we have with Him.

However, God was not only interested in having a covenant with the generation of *Matan Torah*, but also with future generations:

> both with those who are standing here with us this day before the Lord our God and with those who are not with us here this day.
>
> *Deuteronomy 29:13*

This means that a fundamental part of our covenant with God, contracted as a People, consists in the *morashah*, in properly and accurately conveying the memory of the laws and principles we experienced at Sinai, as well as the Sinai experience itself. However, in a world of entropy, memory is also subject to deterioration. That is why education plays a fundamental role for *Ạm Yisra'el*:

> But take utmost care and watch yourselves scrupulously, so that you do not forget the things that you saw with your own eyes and so

1 Deuteronomy 16:3

> that they do not fade from your mind as long as you live. And make them known to your children and to your children's children.
>
> *Deuteronomy 4:9*

The event of the Jewish calendar that embraces more than any other the value of education, of the transmission of an identity and of our history, is the Pesaḥ *Seder*. Throughout the *Seder* we have different pedagogical mechanisms to connect at different levels with the experience of *Yeṣiat Miṣraim*. The first is to generate strategies for children, young people, and anyone present to get involved through questions concerning the meaning of the *Seder* Night — *Ma Nishtana HaLaila Hazeh*? This is achieved by doing strange things, such as taking the *qe'ạra* to another place or hiding the *afiqoman*, generating curiosity and interest.

The second and most important aspect of the *Seder* Night is the narrative vehicle, *Sipur Yeṣiat Miṣraim*, in which we are required to recount the event of the Exodus and delve into its details. Not only do we have to tell the facts, but we must tell them narratively from *genut* to *shebaḥ* — from contempt to praise. This is of great relevance, since the way in which human beings integrate information in a personal way is through stories.

On the other hand, the Pesaḥ *Seder* also consists of multisensory vehicles that connect us with the original experience of leaving Egypt. The *Qorban Pesaḥ* requires many halakhic details to be performed correctly, including: cooking it roasted; not breaking a single bone; eating it with shoes on, and so forth. HaRaMBa"M in *More Nebukhim* explains that all these detailed *halakhot* generate the remembrance of the haste with which *Ạm Yisra'el* left Egypt, reminding us the way in which the original *Seder* Night was celebrated. (For example; someone in a hurry cannot afford to slow-cook meat in its own juice). The *Qorban Pesaḥ* ritual not only fulfills the function of reinforcing the story of the rushed Passover ceremonies, but also fulfills the function of their tangible reenactment. The same happens with the ritual consumption of the *maṣa* and the *maror*.

Not only is the *Seder* experience a "generative process" in which we evoke our past, relive it, and pass it on to the next generation; rather, the very story we use as the text for the *Haggada* is testimony that as a people we do not educate through History, but by *Zikaron*.

Naturally we would think that *Sipur Yeṣiat Miṣraim* is fulfilled by reciting the *pesuqim* of *Sefer Shemot*, the *pesuqim* which narrate what happened "in real time"; however, the sages established in the *Haggada* that we recount it with some *pesuqim* from *Sefer Debarim* (specifically, the declaration that we made when carrying the *bikurim* to the *Bet Hamiqdash*) with which *Yeṣiat Miṣraim* was remembered, generation after generation, since the entrance to *Ereṣ Yisra'el*:

וְעָנִיתָ וְאָמַרְתָּ לִפְנֵי יְהוָה אֱלֹהֶיךָ אֲרַמִּי אֹבֵד אָבִי וַיֵּרֶד מִצְרַיְמָה וַיָּגָר שָׁם בִּמְתֵי מְעָט וַיְהִי־שָׁם לְגוֹי גָּדוֹל עָצוּם וָרָב׃ וַיָּרֵעוּ אֹתָנוּ הַמִּצְרִים וַיְעַנּוּנוּ וַיִּתְּנוּ עָלֵינוּ עֲבֹדָה קָשָׁה׃ וַנִּצְעַק אֶל־יְהוָה אֱלֹהֵי אֲבֹתֵינוּ וַיִּשְׁמַע יְהוָה אֶת־קֹלֵנוּ וַיַּרְא אֶת־עָנְיֵנוּ וְאֶת־עֲמָלֵנוּ וְאֶת־לַחֲצֵנוּ וַיּוֹצִאֵנוּ יְהוָה מִמִּצְרַיִם בְּיָד חֲזָקָה וּבִזְרֹעַ נְטוּיָה וּבְמֹרָא גָּדֹל וּבְאֹתוֹת וּבְמֹפְתִים׃

You shall then recite as follows before your God: "My father was a fugitive Aramean. He went down to Egypt with meager numbers and sojourned there; but there he became a great and very populous nation. The Egyptians dealt harshly with us and oppressed us; they imposed heavy labor upon us. We cried to the Lord, the God of our ancestors, and the Lord heard our plea and saw our plight, our misery, and our oppression. And the Lord freed us from Egypt by a

> mighty hand, by an outstretched arm and awesome power, and by signs and portents.
>
> *Deuteronomy 26:5–8*

Why did the Ḥakhamim establish that we must fulfill the *miṣva* of *Sipur Yeṣiat Miṣraim* through these *pesuqim* written forty years after leaving Egypt? Would it not be more accurate to use the *pesuqim* that narrate what happened "in real time" and describe everything in much more detail?

Morasha, not History. Our National Memory of the Exodus and the profound relationship we have with it is much more than a mere memory of its historical details. The narrative that has accompanied us since ancient times from *genut* to *shebaḥ*, from slavery to Freedom, from *ạboda zara* to faithfulness in God, One and All-mighty — that is the Living Memory of *Ạm Yisra'el.*

✦

How Long Did *Yisra'el* Serve in Egypt?

Matthew Miller

Matthew Miller is a Canadian by birth and a global citizen at heart. He has a passion for language and biblical studies, having completed a BA in Linguistics and Jewish Studies at McGill University and an MA focused on Hebrew Linguistics at Queen Mary University in London. He lives in Chicago with his wife Georgia and daughter Aviya and works as a market research analyst at G2. He also has the privilege and honour of working with Rabbi Efrem Goldberg and The Ḥabura on their content and media distribution.

How long were the Israelites in Egypt? If one were to ask any Jewish person with a decent Jewish education, chances are that they would tell you that the servitude lasted for 210 years. This extended period is certainly lengthy, yet it does not match the description provided in the Bible itself. Here are two texts, the first from Genesis and the second from Exodus:

> And He said to Abram, Know well that your offspring shall be strangers in a land not theirs, and they shall be enslaved and oppressed for four hundred years.
>
> *Genesis 15:13*

> The length of time that the Israelites lived in Egypt was four hundred and thirty years.
>
> *Exodus 12:40*

The first text describes God's address to Abraham at the time of the covenant between the parts, and the second is taken from the Exodus narrative itself. In both texts the duration of the period of Israelite residence in Egypt seems to be approximately double the commonly provided figure. How, then, did 210 become the commonly accepted number, and wherefore went the straightforward meaning of the Biblical text?

It all goes back to RaSH"I

One does not need to conduct any extensive research to find the source of this oft-quoted figure. The idea that the Egyptian servitude lasted 210 years is ubiquitous in rabbinic literature.

The Talmud, for example, states:

> Rabbi Elazar said: For what reason was Abraham our Patriarch punished and his children enslaved to Egypt for 210 years? Because he made a draft [*angarya*] of Torah scholars.
>
> *Nedarim 32a*

RaSH"I explains:

> ...from the birth of Isaac until Israel left Egypt was a period of 400 years...They were in Egypt 210 years — corresponding to the numerical value of the word רדו.

He then states that one cannot interpret the Biblical text literally. He notes:

> ...if, however, you say that they were in Egypt 400 years — well, Kohath was one of those who went down to Egypt with Jacob; go and add up the years of Kohath (130), those of Amram (137), and the 80 years that Moses was old when Israel left Egypt, and you only have about 350, and you really have to deduct all the years that Kohath lived after Amram was born, and those that Amram lived after the birth of Moses.
>
> *Commentary to Genesis 15:13*

In other words, RaSH"I says that the numbers do not add up, and it cannot be the case that the Israelites were in Egypt for 400 years. Although others accept the rabbinic figure of a 200-year Egyptian servitude, its popularity nowadays can no doubt be attributed to Rashi and his ubiquitous nature. Incidentally, RaSH"I resolves the 400 *vs.* 430 year discrepancy, commenting that "there had been 30 years since that decree made at 'the covenant between the parts' until the birth of Isaac."[1]

We should also note the approach of RaMBa"N, who contends Genesis 15:13 does not purport to lay out the number of years the Israelites were in exile:

> This is a verse that is to be transposed, its purport being that "thy seed shall be a stranger for four hundred years in a land that is not theirs, and they shall enslave them, and they shall afflict them." He has thus not specified the length of the period of servitude and affliction.
>
> *Commentary to Genesis 15:13*

We cannot ignore the plain sense of the text

Although RaSH"I's resolution is compelling, inasmuch as it raises a legitimate problem with the text and attempts to resolve it, it is not the only way to evaluate and resolve the commentators' dilemma. Indeed, as Ibn Ezra and other *pashṭanim* taught us, we must seek to understand the *peshaṭ* of the text and not ignore its plain sense meaning. If the text tells us that the Israelites were in Egypt for 430 years, then we must at least attempt to understand how this could be the case. The Septuagint translation stated that the 400 years were spent in Egypt, but also *in other lands*.[2] The Samaritan Pentateuch amended the text to include residence in the *land of Canaan*. We do not distort the plain meaning of the text in such a manner, nor can we be satisfied with the approach of RaSH"I who begins the count from the birth of Isaac, for this is not in accordance with the plain sense of the text.

---

1 Commentary to Exodus 12:40

2 As reported in *Megillah* 9a

Our difficulty is compounded when we read Genesis 15:16: "And they shall return here in the fourth generation, for the iniquity of the Amorites is not yet complete."

What is this mysterious fourth generation and how is that to be reconciled with the 400 years referenced but a few verses earlier? Some commentators, like Ibn Ezra, understand that this passage refers to the four generations that lived in the land of Egypt:

> And so it was: Kohath, Amram, Moses and Aaron were strangers in Egypt. Their children, who were the fourth generation, returned to the land of Cana'an.
>
> *Abraham Ibn Ezra, commentary to Genesis 15:16*

The textual inconsistencies are surmountable

One should note that there is no contradiction between Genesis 15:13 and 15:16, for neither passage mentions a specific or exact location. Ibn Ezra maintains that 400 years would be calculated from the time of the "covenant between the parts", and that the "fourth generation" would be calculated from the beginning of the Egyptian servitude. RaShBa"M understands the verses to be expressing the same idea, as a generation is equivalent to a hundred years. He writes[3] that the reason God mentioned the fourth generation was to explain to Abram why the delay in fulfilling His promise would require 400 years. Because a generation was thought to be equivalent to a period of 100 years, "four generations" would be understood as a period of 400 years.[4]

---

3 Commentary to Genesis 15:16

4 See *Ẹdiyot* 12:9

However, the challenge comes when one reads Exodus 12:40, for this verse explicitly references a sojourn in Egypt that lasted more than 400 years.

Can one understand that there was a 400-year sojourn in Egypt that only spanned four generations? From a genealogical perspective, this seems highly dubious. Troubled by the apparent internal contradiction in Genesis 15 between verse 13 (400 years) and verse 15 (four generations), an opinion in the *Mekhilta* proposes that they are in fact contradictory, but refer to different outcomes based on how the people will act:

> Ribi says: One verse states: "and they shall serve them and they shall afflict them four hundred years," and another, "and the fourth generation will return here." How are these two verses to be reconciled? If they repent, I will redeem them by generations (Abraham, Isaac, Jacob, and the tribes). If not, I will redeem them by years.
>
> *Mekhilta 12:40*

SHaDa"L to the rescue

Nevertheless, there were those who took Exodus 12:40 at face value, such as R. Samuel David Luzzatto (SHaDa"L, 1800-1865). The illustrious Italian exegete read the text anew, with fresh perspectives. He notes that: "Perforce, we must say that the Bible omitted some generations between Kohath and Amram."[5]

He makes this judgment based on the fact that Numbers 3:28 notes that Kohath was numbered at 8,600. However, with only four sons, that would mean that each son had 2,150 sons. Even if one were to accept the Midrashic tradition that says that the women gave birth to sextuplets, this is very difficult to maintain.

[5] Commentary to Exodus 6:20

SHaDa"L remarks based on I.B. Koppe, that having a full 430 years in Egypt makes it much easier to explain the nation's growth to 600,000 men. According to his understanding, Levi, Kohath, and Amram were not successive generations, but rather, there were other less important generations in between them which the Bible did not mention.

SHaDa"L understands the "fourth generation" in accordance with RaSH"I's approach:

> Jacob went down to Egypt. Go and count up his generations: Judah, Perez, Hezron — and Caleb (whose father Jephuneh is identified with Hezron, see Sotah 11b) was amongst those who entered the land of Canaan.
>
> *RaSH"I, commentary to Genesis 15:16*

Conclusion

Now that we have examined the complicated and problematic issues inherent in this text: What should one do the next time someone asks: "How long were the Jews in Egypt?" I suggest that the response to that question should be that it depends on *who* one asks.

That response would be the most honest one of all, as there are a variety of different ways to understand these texts. Whether one is examining the apparent contradictions within Genesis 15, the issue in Exodus 12:40, or the short Levitical line, one must work hard to square the circle and understand these texts in a harmonious fashion.

The Torah has "Seventy Faces," each approach and each commentator attempting to read and reconcile disparate texts in diverse ways. Whether we adopt the approach of RaSH"I, Rabbi Samuel David Luzzato, or any other commentator, we should always remember that the ultimate aim and focus of our study is to improve our understanding of God's Word and world.

✦

Nisayon at Mara: From Mental *Ạbdut* to *Ḥerut*

Eli Shaubi

Eli Shaubi is currently a PhD student of Arabic Language and Literature at Hebrew University, writing on the Maimonidean roots in the thought of R. Abraham ben HaRaMBa"M. He recently served as the Translation Editor of a new Hebrew edition of Maimonides' *Guide for the Perplexed*, and is currently working on several projects, including a forthcoming English translation of the Maimonides' *Introduction to the Mishna*, as well as working with Professor Bernard Septimus on a new English translation and commentary on the Maimonides' *Sefer ha-Madda'*, and with Professor Tzvi Langermann on publishing a 15th century Yemenite commentary to *The Guide*, with both English and Hebrew translations. Eli is the Head of the Israel Division of The Ḥabura, and currently lives in Jerusalem with his wife Meital and son Ori.

A simile I frequently use in describing the Torah, is that it is akin to a workout regimen for strengthening the muscle of free-will. The stronger a person's free-will muscle, the more he is capable of acting in accordance with his will. In fact, what distinguishes man from the animal is man's potential to *choose* his actions, as opposed to having his base instincts dictate his actions to him. The actualisation of that potential is what is meant by man's *ṣelem*.[1] Man may choose to neglect that regimen and allow his muscle to atrophy, at which point he is essentially no different from an animal. Or he may become a prophet, our equivalent of a world-class athlete.

As slaves in Egypt, the Pharaoh commanded us to perform *his* will, for *his* own personal benefit at our expense; we were slaves to his will. Exercising *our* will, therefore, would take the form of insubordination: refusing to obey his command; breaking the chains of bondage; and demanding freedom. As servants of God, in comparison, His will, as expressed in the Law, is for *our* benefit. The Law, therefore, represents *our* will as much as it represents His. As such, exercising *our* will takes the form of obeying the Law and performing His commandments.

The commandments, as opposed to our base instincts, are an imposed, external directive, and our performing them is a product of our *choosing* to perform them. Our animalistic drives, on the other hand, internally pervert our mental focus, such that without refocusing, we let them dictate our actions to us.

---

1 See *Mishneh Torah, Hilkhot Yesodé HaTorah* 4:8, where the *ṣelem* is presented as only referring to the *ṣura* of the human who is *shalem be-daạto*. The *ṣelem* is not the *nefesh* itself, which is present in all men, but rather is *ṣurat ha-nefesh*. That is, the *ṣelem* does not exist in people *a priori*, but is rather acquired as one develops his mind. What all men possess is the *potential* to acquire that perfection.

Acting on our drives, therefore, is the *relinquishing* of choice,[2] and it is choice that makes us human. One measure of our humanity, therefore, is our ability to perform His commandments, while the opposite may be measured by the extent to which we fail in performing our will.

The Pharaoh enslaved us to act against our will and, in a similar manner, the atrophy of our free-will "muscle" also enslaves us to act against our will. In the latter case, however, it is we who enslave ourselves, as a product of our own choices. This freedom from mental enslavement is the *ḥerut* that the Torah provides us: freedom under the Law. In fact, it is this principle of choice, and of man's potential to make himself a *real* human, that is the foundation for having a Torah altogether.[3] With this in mind, we may contemplate the interim period between the Exodus and the reception of the Torah at Mount Sinai, and examine what steps were taken in making the transition from *ạbdut* to *ḥerut*.

Israel's first encampment, after three days of walking through the desert, was in *Mara*,[4] followed by several other encampments. Scattered throughout are several *nisyonot*, by which God "challenges" Israel (and by which they, sometimes, "challenge" Him, much to Moses' chagrin). At *Mara*, the Torah

---

2 See *Moreh Nebukhim* 3:8, where RaMBa"M explains that all disobedience and sin is consequent upon man's *matter*, whereas all his virtues are consequent upon his form.

3 See *Moreh Nebukhim* 3:32, and Ḥakham José Faur's *Homo Mysticus*, p. 131.

4 See Numbers 33:8, where *Mara* is actually listed as Israel's fifth encampment since leaving *Ra'ạmses* in Egypt. The previous encampments occurred in the interim period after the Pharaoh had allowed Israel to leave, but before his decision to chase after the nation, prior to the parting of the Sea. In this sense, those encampments are all pre-Exodus encampments, *Mara* being the first to occur after completely leaving Egypt's grip.

states: "There, did [God] establish for [Israel] *ḥoq u-mishpaṭ*, and there, did He challenge them."[5]

To what *ḥoq* and *mishpaṭ* is the Torah here referring, and what does *nisayon* mean in this context?

Again later, regarding God's gift of the manna to Israel, we read:

> God said to Moses, "I am now going to bring down sustenance for you from the skies, and the nation shall thereupon go out and gather the daily portion on its day, so that I may challenge them, as to whether they will follow my instruction or not."[6]
>
> *Exodus 15:4*

What does "challenging" mean in this context? The significance of this question is heightened if we note that the same phrase is used with regard to Abraham at *Ạqedat Yiṣḥaq*, where we read that God "challenged" Abraham:[7]

> For now I know that you are God-fearing, having not spared from Me your one and only son.[8]
>
> *Genesis 22:12*

Are these "challenges" necessary for God to know something that He did not know previously? That, of course, is preposterous. RaMBa"M resolves this difficulty for us:

> Know that the purpose and meaning of every *nisayon* that is mentioned in the Torah is none other than to make known to man what it is that he ought to do, or what convictions he must have.

---

5 Exodus 15:25

6 Exodus 15:4

7 Genesis 22:1

8 Genesis 22:12

> The meaning of a *nisayon*, then, is that some action be done, when the intent is not for that particular action, but rather that it be an example to be imitated and emulated.[9]
>
> *Moreh Nebukhim 3:24*

A *nisayon* is not concerned with the-specific deed in question, be it giving Isaac as an offering, or gathering the manna. The act is merely a representation of the *choice* behind that proper act, that is to be *habituated* in the mind of the person, such that the choice may be repeated in similar contexts. The way in which the Torah strengthens the "muscle" of free-will is by commanding individuals to perform actions that go *against* one's nature. By nature, man is wont to eat what he likes and have sex whenever he likes, as those activities are physically enjoyable to him. The Torah commands man to exercise his will, such that he not be a slave to his nature, but rather *ben ḥorin* to act as he wills, as we explained above. The *nisayon*, then, is a "challenge" in the sense that it is a moment of choice. It is not a test for God to know what man will choose, but rather an opportunity for man to choose to be free or to be a slave.[10] Thus RaMBa"M states:

> The meaning of *nasotekha* can also be "to habituate you," as in His saying (Deuteronomy 28:56):
>
> "הרכה בך והענגה אשר לא נסתה כף רגלה הצג על הארץ מהתענג ומרך"
>
> "The pampered and delicate woman whose sole was not habituated/accustomed to stepping on land, being so delicate and tender."
>
> *Moreh Nebukhim 3:24*

9 *Moreh Nebukhim* 3:24

10 Likewise, a *nes*, in addition to "a banner," can mean "a milestone" in one's life.

We may now understand the purpose of the interim period between the Exodus from Egypt and the reception of the Torah at Sinai. The several *nisyonot* mentioned therein, served the purpose of presenting Israel with an opportunity, a moment of choice, in which Israel could be habituated in some proper choice. But in which kind of choice? Let us re-examine the *pesuqim*, first at *Mara*:

> ויצעק אל יהוה ויורהו יהוה עץ וישלך אל המים וימתקו המים שם שם לו חק ומשפט ושם נסהו: ויאמר אם שמוע תשמע לקול יהוה אלהיך והישר בעיניו תעשה והאזנת למצותיו ושמרת כל חקיו כל המחלה אשר שמתי במצרים לא אשים עליך כי אני יהוה רפאך:
>
> And he cried out to the Lord, and the Lord showed him a piece of wood, and he sent it upon the face of the waters, and the waters were sweetened. There, He established for them [Israel] *ḥoq u-mishpaṭ*, and there, did He challenge them. And He said, If you shall listen to the voice of the Lord your God, and shall do the upright in His eyes, and you shall hear His commandments, and you shall keep all His statutes, all the disease that I placed within Egypt I shall not place upon you, for I am the Lord, your Healer.

Exodus 15:25-26

And regarding the manna:

> ויאמר יהוה אל משה הנני ממטיר לכם לחם מן השמים ויצא העם ולקטו דבר יום ביומו למען אנסנו הילך בתורתי אם לא:
>
> And the Lord said to Moses, Behold, I am raining down for you bread from the Heavens, and the nation shall go out and collect each day's matter on its day, in order that I may challenge them (*anasenu*), if they shall walk in My Torah or not.

Exodus 16:4

Both *nisyonot* served the same purpose: to habituate Israel *in the performance of His commandments.* The content of the commandment, at this point, is irrelevant, so much so that in the first instance, the Torah does not even bother telling us what the command was, beyond simply stating *ḥoq u-mishpaṭ*. What matters is that the people of Israel, after a long bondage in Egypt, begin exercising their free-will muscle once again, in preparation for the reception of the Torah.[11] R. Abraham ben HaRaMBa"M sheds light on this in his comment to Exodus 15:25:

> The "challenge" of The Waters of Mara was to make clear to them that for the path of adhering to the Torah, one needs to be capable of struggling [against one's instincts] (*mujāhada*)[12] and breaking loose of habits.[13] "*Ve-sham nissahu*" bears two possible explanations: The first is that [*lenassot*] has the meaning of habituation, whereby the meaning [of the verse] would be that "There, they became habituated in struggle, restraint, and trust."

The process of bringing freedom to Israel is a long and difficult one, and they fail several times (as in the case of the manna, about which Moses is swift in rebuking them). It contains numerous steps on the way, each step presenting a new opportunity, and a new moment of choice on the path to true *ḥerut*. That choice is the difference between real life and death, as Moses tells us at the end of the Torah, "See, I have placed before you today, life and goodness, or

11 Similarly, RaMBa"M placed *Hilkhot Deọt* prior to *Hilkhot Talmud Torah* in the *Mishneh Torah.*

12 *Mujāhada*, literally "struggle," is defined by R. Abraham in his *Kifāya* (Rosenblatt, 2:312) as: "That a person's mind and intellect overcome their desires and nature."

13 Because all habituation in certain choices requires breaking loose of prior habits.

death and badness...You shall choose life, so that you may live."[14]

✦

[14] Deuteronomy 30:15-20

Moshe's Absence, Our Presence

Daniel Osen

Daniel Osen is from the New York City metropolitan area, and is currently pursuing a degree in Jewish Studies (with a focus on Bible and Near Eastern Studies) at Yeshiva University. He has previously studied at Yeshivat Torah v'Avodah, the Hebrew University of Jerusalem, and Bar-Ilan University.

The fact that Moses' name does not appear once in the actual text of the *Haggada* is one that is commonly repeated. The reality is that the central human agent in the Exodus, Moses, makes a brief cameo appearance in a passing exegetical statement by R. Yossei HaGelili, which does not even appear in older versions of the ritual text. Moses' absence from the text is conspicuous. Imagine a recounting of the American Civil War that does not mention Abraham Lincoln: yes, it could be done but it would be an unusual way to recount the historical event. It is hard to believe that the editors of the *Haggada* simply forgot the significance of Moses. Rather, his non-prominence is crucial to understanding the role of Moses in our history as well as the nature of Pesaḥ.

In Deuteronomy, it is unequivocally stated that Moses was unique amongst the Prophets in his interface with God (Deuteronomy 34:10). Even without this verse, Moses track record throughout the Torah is more than sufficient to justify this claim. From leading the Children of Israel out of Egypt, to serving as the intermediary between the people and God at Sinai, Moses served as the leader of the Children of Israel in nearly every capacity conceivable. Nonetheless, Moses constantly found himself being hounded and attacked by the people for doing his job properly and competently. Moses, of course, was human and his response to the stubbornness and ingratitude of the people he led ate at his psyche, but he never fully abandoned the task he had been assigned.

It cannot be emphasised enough that Moses had no interest in being a national leader. In a series of narratives in Genesis, Noah and the Patriarchs answer God's call immediately and affirmatively, whereas, initially, Moses rejects the Master of the Universe's command.

In Moses' own words:

> Who am I, that I should go to the Pharaoh? Shall I take the Children of Israel from out of Egypt?[1]
>
> *Exodus 3:11*

Moses says that he views himself as uniquely unqualified to lead the Children of Israel out of Egypt because he lacks the prerequisite pedigree for the job. Even after God reassures Moses by providing him with a series of signs to convince the people of his legitimacy, Moses still insists that he is unfit for the task at hand:

> Please, O Lord, I am not a man of words, not from yesterday, nor from the day before, nor from now that You have spoken to Your servant, for I am heavy of mouth and heavy of tongue.
>
> *Exodus 4:10*

Moses – the human with the most dialogue in the Torah – claims that he is a poor orator and lacks the refinement and precision of language that is required of a leader. God provides his famous reply:

> Who places a mouth for a man? Or Who makes one mute, or deaf, or seeing, or blind? Is it not I, the Lord?
>
> *Exodus 4:11*

These words serve as an unassailable refutation of Moses' concerns. While Moses is tasked with the role of directly

[1] Exodus 3:11

speaking with Pharaoh and leading the Children of Israel, he is not doing so in a vacuum. Moses' fears about his supposed lack of qualifications for the task at hand are the exact reason why he is suited to lead. Guided by his unrivaled sense of humility,[2] Moses' sense of leadership is not informed by grandiose ideals of his role in capital-H "History" much less any desire for self-aggrandisement. Instead, he acts as a leader in the purest sense of the term; he works to guide the public towards their goal, he enforces the Law as needed, and addresses their problems to the best of his abilities, all with the knowledge that the nature of his mission transcends both himself and those he has been assigned to lead.

The *pasuq* quoted by R. Yossi haGelili that is the *Haggada*'s only mention of Moshe doubles down on this point:

> And Israel saw the great hand which the Lord wielded against Egypt, and the nation feared the Lord, and had faith in the Lord, and in Moses, His servant.
>
> *Exodus 14:31*

After crossing the Red Sea, the Children of Israel had come to embrace and revere God, and that enabled them to accept Moses' role as leader. In other words, in that moment the Israelites were able to accept Moses' role as the servant of God. Moses is merely the means, whereas God is the end. Therefore, Moses being absent from our annual recounting of *Yeṣiat Miṣrayim* is perfectly logical. While the Biblical text treats him as the central human agent of change in the Exodus narrative, this is of secondary importance in our national recounting of these events.

---

2 See Numbers 12:3

From the very institution of this holiday, the first *miṣva* given to the Children of Israel, each and every household is commanded to take their own lamb to slaughter. There is no stand-in or intermediary to inaugurate the holiday, the obligation is incumbent on each household. This is true in our time as well, albeit in a different fashion. Incorporated into our Pesaḥ *sedarim,* the Mishnah in *Pesaḥim* best encapsulates the essence of the experience *vis à vis* the words of Rabban Gamliel:

> Any individual who did not state these three items on Pesaḥ did not fulfil his obligation: *Pesaḥ*, *Maṣa*, and *Maror*.
>
> *Pesaḥim 10:5*

Each of these three items is connected to the events being commemorated: the *Pesaḥ* to the fact that God passed over the houses of the Children of Israel that were marked with the blood of the *Qorban Pesaḥ*, the *Maṣa* on the basis that our ancestors were redeemed from Egypt, and *Maror* because the Egyptians' embitterment of the lives of our forefathers. While this list is rooted in the *pesuqim* surrounding this holiday, it seems odd that there is a *requirement* to explain the reason why these objects are on our tables. This oddity is clarified immediately thereafter:

> In every generation, one is required to view himself as if he left Egypt, as the verse states: "And you shall tell your son on that day, saying, Because of this which the Lord did for me when I went out of Egypt.

Rabban Gamliel presents us with the obligation to view ourselves as if we had personally left Egypt, bolstered by our obligation to explain the significance of the *Pesaḥ, Maṣa, and Maror.* The symbolism of those three items provides the framework for our retellings of the Exodus, and squarely establishes that eternal obligation as one that is focused on the events as those of national memory, rather than as a celebration of a particular person. Moshe's name is absent — not because he is unimportant — but because he is not us.

There is, of course, a seemingly glaring flaw in my thesis. The assumptions about the Torah's and the *Haggada*'s relationship to mortal men sounds perfectly fine and well. However, this fails to account for a significant piece of the data which is the *Haggada*'s preoccupation with recounting the various teachings of the *Tannaim*. The *Haggada* seems to be focused on the discussions of these specific men. While at face value this may appear to be a tremendous threat to my argument, it misconstrues the role of the *Tannaim* in the *Haggada*. In 2022 we struggle with the intrinsic challenges presented by trying to envision ourselves as participants in a moment in history three thousand years in the past, predicated on experiences that are completely foreign to us. Ḥazal were no less perplexed by this challenge and using the tools they had, they attempted to relive the Exodus as best they could through various *derashot*. In other words, Ḥazal struggled with that same basic challenge and laid out a series of *derashot* as a foundation-text to enable us to see ourselves as if we had personally left Egypt. Therefore, the point is not to exalt or sanctify the people who provided us with these teachings, but rather to have those texts inform our own retellings of the story. Just as the sages used the tools at their disposal to relive the Exodus in the manner they saw fit, we have the obligation to do so through our own intellectual apparatus.

While it would be a gross historical error to state that Moses was irrelevant to *yeṣiat miṣrayim*, in the context of the *Seder* it would almost be correct. As a national event, having it tied to any one person would undermine our capacity to appreciate those events as individuals, as forever we would find ourselves in the shadow of the great man who helped facilitate the Exodus. By eliminating that element, it allows for each and every one of us to see ourselves in the Exodus.

The *pasuq* that this obligation stems from has a crucial ambiguity which is essential to framing the nature of this obligation. The word "this"/זה is problematic because it is unclear what the subject of this word is. RaSH"I and Ibn Ezra offer similar explanations and interpret the text as signifying "for the sake of the *miṣvot* that we are obliged to observe both now and always." On the other hand, RaMBa"N and RaShB"AM propose that the problematic word means "that" leading to the reading of the *pasuq* as: "And you will tell your son on that day to say, [this entire proceeding] is for the sake of that which God did for me in my leaving Egypt."

While these competing interpretations each have their own strengths and weakness, they ultimately arrive at the same conclusion. This entire enterprise is made worthless without establishing that we are commemorating these events theocentrically, whether it be by tying them to God's deeds in Egypt or to the Torah that He gave us. Without this anchor, the Seder becomes a vapid, purposeless meal.

Immediately after witnessing the drowning of entire Egyptian army in the waters of the Red Sea, Moshe and the Children of Israel sing a song of praise to God extolling His greatness and feats. In a similar vein Rabban Gamliel concludes his set of obligations at the Seder with the following:

> לְפִיכָךְ אֲנַחְנוּ חַיָּבִין לְהוֹדוֹת, לְהַלֵּל, לְשַׁבֵּחַ, לְפָאֵר, לְרוֹמֵם, לְהַדֵּר, לְבָרֵךְ, לְעַלֵּה, וּלְקַלֵּס, לְמִי שֶׁעָשָׂה לַאֲבוֹתֵינוּ וְלָנוּ אֶת כָּל הַנִּסִּים הָאֵלּוּ, הוֹצִיאָנוּ מֵעַבְדוּת לְחֵרוּת, מִיָּגוֹן לְשִׂמְחָה, וּמֵאֵבֶל לְיוֹם טוֹב, וּמֵאֲפֵלָה לְאוֹר גָּדוֹל, וּמִשִּׁעְבּוּד לִגְאֻלָּה.
>
> Therefore, we are obligated to thank, praise, laud, glorify, exalt, lavish, bless, raise high, and acclaim He Who performed – for our forefathers and for us – all of these miracles: He took us out of bondage to freedom, from anguish to happiness, and from mourning to a day of goodness, and from darkness to a great light, and from slavery to redemption.
>
> *Haggada, Magid*

As we sit around our own *Seder* tables, we conclude our commemoration of the Exodus in the exact same way our ancestors did: by giving thanks to God in acknowledgement of what He has done for each and every one of us, as members of *Ạm Yisra'el,* as only we can do as ourselves. *Ḥag Sameaḥ!*

✦

Signals and Signets: The Ancient Egyptian Roots of *Tefillin*

Jacob Chereskin

Jacob Chereskin is a native of Chicago, and currently lives in Washington D.C. with his wife and daughter. He is a graduate of the George Washington University's Elliott School of International Affairs and has studied at Yeshivat Machon Meir in Jerusalem.

For observant Jewish men, our *tefillin* are a vital tool to aid in our worship of God. However, those outside our nation, as well as some of our brethren, are often confused by the significance of this practice. Like many practices of the ancient times, the act of tying scroll-filled boxes with leather straps on our arms and heads is something completely beyond the frame of reference for many people.

For those of us who follow in the footsteps of *Ḥakhme Sepharad*, it is imperative for us to avoid the fallacy of judging our ancient law based on the standards of contemporary society. As with many of the *miṣvot* of the Torah, it is critical to understand the temporal and cultural context in which our law was transmitted.

In *Moreh Nebukhim*, HaRaMBa"M tells his student, Yosef ben Yehuda, of his attempts to understand the *miṣvot* according to the cultures of the time, particularly the Sabeans:[1]

> וכל שנעלם טעמו מרוב החוקים אינו אלא להרחיק מעבודה זרה. ואותם הפרטים אשר נעלם ממני טעמם ולא ידעתי מה תועלתם, סיבת הדבר לפי שאין הדברים הנשמעים כנראים, ולפיכך אין בכדי מה שידעתי אני משיטות ה"צאבה" ממה ששמעתי מן הספרים, כמו ידיעת מי שראה מעשיהם לנוכח, ובפרט שאותן ההשקפות כבר אבדו זה אלפים שנה או יותר.

That I cannot explain some details of the above laws or show their use in owing to the fact that what we hear from others is not so clear

1 The Sabeans were an ancient pagan sect, said to be named after *Sabi*, son of Enoch. Their creed comprehended the worship of one God, the Governor and Creator of all things, who was to be addressed through a mediator, whose office was to be performed by pure and invisible spirits. In his commentary on *Ạboda Zara* 4:7, HaRaMBa"M states: "the Sabians were the nation that Abraham our forefather, peace be upon him, came from yet disagreed with their mistake and their faulty argument."

> as that which we see with our own eyes. Thus, my knowledge of the Sabean doctrines, which I derived from books, is not as complete as the knowledge of those who have witnessed the public practice of those idolatrous customs, especially as they have been out of practice and entirely extinct for two thousand years.[2]

As we examine the laws pertaining to one of the most commonly practiced rituals today, we will cross reference the culture of the Egyptians, whose own beliefs and practices permeated the lives of our ancestors.

When examining the sources for *miṣvat tefillin* in the written Torah, the Talmud and halakhic compendiums such as the *Mishneh Torah* and *Shulḥan Ạrukh* cite Deuteronomy, which prescribes this *miṣva* in order to maintain awareness of God:

> Bind them as a sign on your hand and let them serve as a symbol (טוטפות) between your eyes.
>
> *Deuteronomy 6:8*

> And you shall place these words of Mine upon your heart and upon your soul, and you shall bind them as a sign on your hand and they shall be a symbol (טוטפות) between your eyes.
>
> *Deuteronomy 11:18*

While we may see the innate connection between *tefillin* and the *mezuza* (another physical reminder of the *Berit*) the particular connection to our ancestors' liberation from Egypt is more perplexing.

Our first step on our journey should be to understand the extremely rare word טוטפות, which itself is linguistically tied to Egypt in the tradition of Ḥazal:

---

2 *Moreh Nebukhim*, 3:49, R. Yosef Qafiḥ Edition, Mossad HaRav Kook

ודכולי עלמא יש אם למקרא והתניא (שמות יג, טז) לטטפת (דברים ו, ח) לטטפת (דברים יא, יח) לטוטפות הרי כאן ארבע דברי ר׳ ישמעאל ר״ע אומר אינו צריך טט בכתפי שתים פת באפריקי שתים:

[The Gemara asks:] **And does everyone actually hold that the vocalisation of the Torah is authoritative? But isn't it taught in a *beraita*:** [With regard to the number of compartments in the phylacteries of the head, the verse states: "It shall be for a sign upon your hand, and] **for *ṭoṭafot*** [between your eyes,"[3] with the word *ṭoṭafot* spelled deficiently, without a second *vav*, in a way that can be read as singular; and again: "They shall be] **for *ṭoṭafot*** [between your eyes,"[4] spelled as a singular word; and again: "They shall be] **for *ṭoṭafot*** [between your eyes,"[5] this time spelled with a second *vav*, in a manner that must be plural?] **There are four mentions of *ṭoṭafot* here** [as the third one is written in the plural and therefore counts as two. Consequently, it is derived that the phylacteries of the head must have four compartments.] **This is the statement of R. Ishmael. Rabbi Akiva says: There is no need** [for this proof, as the requirement of four compartments can be derived from the word *ṭoṭafot* itself: The word] ***ṭaṭ* in the language of the Katfei means two,** and [the word] ***pat* in the language of Afriqi** [also] **means two** [and therefore *ṭoṭafot* can be understood as a compound word meaning: Four. The *beraita* therefore indicates that Rabbi Ishmael holds that not the vocalisation, rather the tradition, of the manner in which the verses in the Torah are written is authoritative.]

Sanhedrin 4b

As explained by R. Akiva, the word טוטפות is a compound word consisting of roots found in Coptic (כתפי) and other African dialects, to which our ancestors would have been exposed while enslaved in Egypt, explaining that both words mean "two,"

3 Exodus 13:16

4 Deuteronomy 6:8

5 *Ibid.* 11:18

alluding to the fourfold division of the *parashiot* in both the head and arm *tefillin*. Another important mention of this word is the use of **טוטפת** in a discussion on acceptable headdresses for women on Shabbat:

> במה אשה יוצאה ובמה אינה יוצאה. לא תצא אשה לא בחוטי צמר ולא בחוטי פשתן ולא ברצועות שבראשה. ולא תטבל בהן עד שתרפם. ולא בטטפת ולא בסנבוטין בזמן שאינן תפורין:
>
> **With what** [items] **may a woman go out** [into the public domain on the Sabbath] **and with what items may she not go out? A woman may neither go out with strings of wool, nor with strings of flax, nor with strips of any other materials that a woman braids in the hair of her head. Nor may a woman immerse** [in a ritual bath] with them [in her hair] **until she loosens them.** [When the strings or strips are tight, the water cannot reach her hair unobstructed, invalidating her immersion. And, likewise,] **a woman may not go out with the ornament called *ṭoṭefet*, nor with *sanbutin* that are not sewn** [into her head covering]**.**
>
> *Shabbat 6a*

While this Egyptian linguistic connection to this *miṣva* is quite interesting, it still does not establish a thematic connection with the Exodus itself. However, when examining Exodus, we see multiple references to *tefillin* in conjunction with God's liberation of the Israelites from Egypt:

> And it shall be for you a sign on your arm and a remembrance between your eyes, in order that the Torah of the Lord shall be in your mouth, for with a strong arm (יד חזקה) did the Lord take you out from Egypt.
>
> *Exodus 13:9*

> And it shall be a sign on your arm and a symbol between your eyes, for with strength of arm (חוק יד) did the Lord take us out from Egypt.
>
> *Exodus 13:16*

The next step in our investigation is to examine the importance of the operative phrases of יד חוקה and חוק יד. Throughout Scripture, these phrases are exclusively used in relation to the Exodus from Egypt, but absent from important events occurring in the Land of Israel.

As many scholars have indeed noted, Egyptian monuments in the New Period used similar phrases centered around commemorations of military victories by Pharaoh Ramesses II, over the enemies of Egypt. One important source for this is the *Kadesh Inscription*, detailing the Egyptian struggle against the Hittites at the Battle of Kadesh in modern-day Syria.[6] In this text, which eerily parallels *Shirat haYam*, Ramesses II is described as possessing a "strong" hand that defeats his enemies and brings about victory for his people.

In artistic depictions of subsequent campaigns, the Pharaoh is depicted adorned in sacred bracelets as he charges into battle against his enemies. These particular objects, often worn in the New Kingdom period by Pharaohs, were blessed in the names of various deities, especially Hathor[7] who appeared in many *stelae*[8] of Ramesside military propaganda as a protector of Pharaoh.[9]

Secondly, another important area to look for parallels for *tefillin* is on the head of the Pharaoh. In battle, Ramesses II was

---

6 Rabbi Dr. Joshua Berman, *Inconsistency in the Torah Ancient Literary Convention and the Limits of Source Criticism*, Oxford University Press (2017), pp. 37-38, 43, 49

7 "Fragment of a Votive Bracelet," National Museums Liverpool

8 A stone or wooden slab, generally taller than it is wide, erected in the ancient world as a monument. The surface of the *stele* often has text, ornamentation, or both. These may be inscribed, carved in relief, or painted.

9 Zahi Hawass, *The Mysteries of Abu Simbel: Ramesses II and the Temples of the Rising Sun*, American University in Cairo Press (2001)

often depicted wearing the common ritual item known as the *uraeus*, a talisman shaped like the snake goddess Wadjet. Commonly placed in both the Pharaonic headdress, known as the *nemes*, and the Pharaonic battle helmet, the *kherpes*, the *uraeus* acted as a talisman representing the divine mission of the Pharaoh, acting as the emanation of the divine on the earth. These objects would act as conduits between the ruler and the deities of Egypt, ensuring continued divine favor for the country.[10]

The motif of a ruler acting as a conduit for the divine through a physical talisman is also present at later points in Israelite history. We can see a possible connection with the holy vestments of Egypt within the story of the aftermath of the death of King Saul:

> So I stood over him and finished him off, for I knew that he would never rise from where he was lying. Then I took the crown from his head and the armlet from his arm, and brought them here to my Lord.
>
> *II Samuel 1:10*

When we see the mentions of the "band" on Saul's head and the "bracelet" upon his arm, a pattern begins to emerge. Pharaohs in Egypt would go into battle wearing amulets signifying their deities—it is quite likely that the kings of Israel did the same in honor of the God of Israel.

Beyond the royal realm, it is also abundantly clear that the general Egyptian populace also had talismans. In the late Iron

---

[10] Marjorie Fisher "A Diplomatic Marriage in the Ramesside Period: Maatheorneferue, Daughter of the Great Ruler of Hatti," *Beyond Hatti: A Tribute to Gary Beckman,* Ed. Billie Jean Collins and Piotr Michalowski, p.107

Age, some members of the Priestly class in Egypt utilised amulets containing messages from oracles granting them help from the gods.[11] This is a probable precursor of the use of scrolls of Torah texts inside *tefillin* in Biblical and Second Temple times. While the scrolls used in *tefillin* throughout history, such as those found at Qumran, may have been in flux, use of the text of the Torah as physical talismans dates back to the 7th Century BCE, as demonstrated by the *Ketef Hinnom Scrolls*.[12] This is another potential indicator of the ancient provenance of the general practice of *tefillin*, if not the format used since the times of Ḥazal.

The presence of a physical totem symbolising a physical connection to a patron deity may in fact have been the basis of the *tefillin*, which constitute the words of Hashem inscribed on the hands of the user. While many might feel that the parallels between *tefillin* with the royal vestments and priestly amulets of Egypt may belittle or cheapen the meaning of this commandment, that is mistaken. The medium may have roots in the pagan practices of old, but the reasoning behind it is totally and fundamentally different.

As Ḥakham Umberto Cassuto mentions in his commentary on the Book of Exodus, the importance of *tefillin* is that we are meant to remember the Exodus by utilising physical means to consistently remember God.

---

11 T. G. Wilfong, "The Oracular Amuletic Decrees: A Question of Length," *Journal of Egyptian Archaeology* XCIX (2013), pp. 295-300

12 Jeremy Smoak, *The Priestly Blessing in Inscription and Scripture: The Early History of Numbers 6:24-26*, Oxford University Press (2015), p.79

> And this thing shall be to you as a sign on your hand and as a remembrance – that is, a memorial – between your eyes so that the law of the Lord may be in your mouth), to wit, that with a strong hand the Lord has brought you out of Egypt. The sign on the hand recalls the "strong hand." Of the form of the sign and the memorial the text gives us no details;
>
> According to Talmudic interpretation, as is well known, the reference is to the precept of the phylacteries. The expression between your eyes certainly means opposite the part between the eyes, that is, on the forehead, which is the Talmudic interpretation of the phrase, and also the [significance] on that the corresponding expressions have in Ugaritic and Syriac.
>
> The law of the Lord...connotes the entire body of precepts connected with the service of the Lord, which you undertook to keep when you dedicated your life to Him on being redeemed from the house of bondage, and which will ever be near to your heart and soul, if you will remember constantly the day when you went forth out of the land of Egypt.
>
> *A Commentary on the Book of Exodus, p.152-153*

By subverting the popular practices of Egypt through submission to the one true God, Judaism has created a practice that has survived over three thousand years of transmission. Without understanding the ancient context behind this practice, many will be hard pressed to understand the beauty of this *miṣva* in its fullest grandeur.

Mo'ạdim leSimḥa.

✦

CONTRIBUTORS

RABBI DR. RATZON ARUSI is Chief Rabbi of Kiryat Ono, a member of Israel's Chief Rabbinate Council, and founder of Halikhot Am Yisra'el Institute. Rabbi Arusi has a Ph.D. in law from Tel Aviv University, and lectures on Jewish law at Bar-Ilan University. He heads Kiryat Ono's rabbinical court for monetary law. A student of Rabbi Yosef Qafih *a"h*, Rabbi Arusi is a respected leader in the Yemenite and Sephardi community, and in the Jewish world at large.

RABBI JOSEPH DWECK is the Senior Rabbi of the S&P Sephardi Community of the UK – the country's oldest Jewish community. He is also the Rosh Bet Midrash of The Ḥabura. He studied in Jerusalem at Yeshivat Hazon Ovadia under the tutelage of the former Sephardi Chief Rabbi of Israel, Rabbi Ovadia Yosef. He has an MA in Jewish education. In his capacity as Senior Rabbi, Rabbi Dweck serves as a President of the Council of Christians and Jews, Deputy President of the London School of Jewish Studies, Ecclesiastical Authority of the Board of Deputies of British Jews, and Standing Committee Member of the Conference of European Rabbis. Visit www.SeniorRabbi.com to find out more about his work and initiatives.

RABBI DR. SAMUEL LEBENS is a research fellow in the philosophy department at the University of Haifa, and a dynamic Jewish educator. He has studied at Yeshivat Hakotel, Yeshivat Hamivtar, and Yeshivat Har Etzion. He holds a Ph.D. in philosophy from Birkbeck College (University of London), and held post-doctoral positions at the University of Notre Dame and Rutgers. Rabbi Dr. Lebens is the author of *Principles of Judaism*, published by Oxford University Press.

RABBI YAMIN LEVY is the Senior Rabbi at the Iranian Jewish Center / Beth Hadassah Synagogue in Great Neck, NY. He is the founder and director of the Maimonides Heritage Center based in Israel and New York. He has authored and edited several books and published extensively in English, Hebrew, and Catalan. He published an award-winning novel entitled *Sababa* that deals with the Israeli Arab conflict. Rabbi Yamin Levy has an active YouTube channel and corresponds via email with a learning community around the world.

PROFESSOR Y. TZVI LANGERMANN earned his Ph.D. in History of Science at Harvard University. After serving some fifteen years on the staff of the Institute of Hebrew Manuscripts in Jerusalem, he joined the Department of Arabic at Bar-Ilan University, where he taught until his retirement in September 2019. His latest books are *Sa'd ibn Mansur Ibn Kammuna. Subtle Insights Concerning Knowledge and Practice* (Yale, 2019), and *In and Around Maimonides* (Gorgias Press, 2021).

DAYAN OFER LIVNAT is a Dayan of the Sephardi Beth Din of the United Kingdom. A graduate of the Eretz Hemdah Institute for Advanced Jewish Studies in Jerusalem, Dayan Livnat teaches in a number of programs for training rabbis and dayanim, including the *semikha* and *dayanut* programs run jointly by the Montefiore Endowment and Eretz Hemdah. Dayan Livnat previously served in an artillery unit in the IDF and is currently studying for a PhD in Jewish Studies at University College London.

RABBI YONATAN HALEVY is author of *Yehi Shalom: A Guide to the Laws of Pesaḥ and Kashrut*, the spiritual leader of Kehillat Shaar HaShamayim in San Diego, and the founder of Shiviti. He studied at Ner Israel in Baltimore, and Shehebar Sephardic Centre in Yerushalayim, receiving *semikha* from Rabbi Yaakov Peretz and Rabbi Shelomo Kassin.

RABBI ABRAHAM FAUR is the rabbi of Congregation Ohel David and Shelomo in New York. Rabbi Faur was ordained by Rabbi Mordechai Eliyahu and Rabbi Abraham Shapira. He teaches Talmudic and Rabbinic thinking in accordance with the Andalusian Ḥakhamim, and the teachings of his father, the great Ḥakham Jose Faur *a"h*. Rabbi Faur has also studied various scientific and philosophic disciplines.

RABBI YITZHAK BERDUGO was born and raised in South Florida. After studying at Yeshivat Beth Moshe Chaim (Talmudic University) in Miami Beach, Rabbi Berdugo received his bachelors in Talmudic law and *semikha* under the auspices of the Rosh Yeshiva, Rabbi Yochanan Moshe Zweig *SHeLIṬ"A*. While studying in New York, Rabbi Berdugo also received his *Yoreh Yoreh* from Rabbi Eliyahu Ben Haim, *Rosh Yeshiva* and *Av Bet Din* of *BaDa"Ṣ* Mekor Haim, Queens, NY, followed by a *Qabala* in *sheḥiṭa* and in lung checking. He has written much on Sephardi Halakha in addition to translating the works of great

Sephardi *Rabbanim*. Currently residing in Miami Beach, Florida, Rabbi Berdugo serves as the Rosh Kollel of the Bal Harbour Kollel and is also studying for *Dayanut* qualification through the Eretz Hemdah Institute of Jerusalem and the Montefiore Endowment.

✦

BEN ROTHSTEIN is a student at University College London studying Ancient Languages. He is originally from East Barnet and attended Yeshivat HaKotel for two years. He has been involved with youth activities for many years and currently works with his wife as a youth worker in the community.

RABBI JACK COHEN is the Associate Rabbi at Hampstead Synagogue, in London. He studied in Yeshivat Har Etzion and received *semikha* from both Rabbi Rimon (Mizrachi) and Rabbi Zalman Nechemia Goldberg *a"h*. He has a degree in philosophy from UCL and currently lives in London with his wife and two sons.

MICHOEL CHALK is originally from London and began his yeshiva study at Kerem BeYavne in 2016. Having completed the IDF Hesder programme there, he resides in Israel pursuing a degree in Cognitive Sciences at the Open University while working as a security bodyguard.

SINA KAHEN was born in Iran and moved to England at the age of 3. He works in the Medical Technology and AI industries and is the author of *Ideas* (a series of books on the weekly Torah portion). He studied Biomedical Sciences, has an MBA from Imperial College, and lives in London with his wife Talya and two children. Sina is also the Co-Founder of The Ḥabura.

MIJAL MEDRESH was raised in a family that transmitted a deep love for Torah and Arts. She studied at Midreshet Lindenbaum and Midreshet Rachel V'Chaya and has continued to study Torah ever since. She graduated from film school and has specialised in the areas of screenwriting, directing and editing. Mijal currently lives in Mexico City with her husband Albert Cohen.

MATTHEW MILLER is a Canadian by birth and a global citizen at heart. He has a passion for language and biblical studies, having completed a BA in Linguistics and Jewish Studies at McGill University and an MA focused on Hebrew Linguistics at Queen Mary University in London. He lives in Chicago with his wife Georgia and daughter Aviya and works as a market research analyst at G2. He also has the privilege and honour of working with Rabbi Efrem Goldberg and The Ḥabura on their content and media distribution.

ELI SHAUBI is currently a PhD student of Arabic Language and Literature at Hebrew University, writing on the Maimonidean roots in the thought of R. Abraham ben HaRaMBa"M. He recently served as the Translation Editor of a new Hebrew edition of Maimonides' *Guide for the Perplexed*, and is currently working on several projects, including a forthcoming English translation of the Maimonides' *Introduction to the Mishna*, as well as working with Professor Bernard Septimus on a new English translation and commentary on the Maimonides' *Sefer ha-Madda'*, and with Professor Tzvi Langermann on publishing a 15th century Yemenite commentary to the *Guide*, with both English and Hebrew translations. Eli is the Head of the Israel Division of The Ḥabura, and currently lives in Jerusalem with his wife Meital and son Ori.

DANIEL OSEN is from the New York City metropolitan area, and is currently pursuing a degree in Jewish Studies (with a focus on Bible and Near Eastern Studies) at Yeshiva University. He has previously studied at Yeshivat Torah v'Avodah, the Hebrew University of Jerusalem, and Bar-Ilan University.

JACOB CHERESKIN is a native of Chicago, and currently lives in Washington D.C. with his wife and daughter. He is a graduate of the George Washington University's Elliott School of International Affairs and has studied at Yeshivat Machon Meir in Jerusalem.

✦

MORD MAMAN is from Manchester, UK. When he isn't creating pixel-perfect websites in his role as a Front End Developer, he spends time with his family, enjoys reading books and riding his bike, but not at the same time! He is the Parnas Presidente of the Manchester Congregation of the Spanish and Portuguese Jews.

FREDDIE GRUNSFELD, 16, resides in Brooklyn, NY. He currently attends Davis Renov Stahler Yeshiva High School for Boys, having previously studied at Barkai Yeshiva. He enjoys studying *Miqra*, *Ḥazzanut*, and Arabic music, and has plans to study about the Ancient Near East in an academic setting.

AVNER YESHURUN, 22, was born in Israel and was raised in the sunny Caribbean island of Curaçao. Following his high school education in Miami, he studied at the Hebron Yeshiva in Jerusalem. He is currently studying finance, fintech, and accounting at the University of Miami Herbert School of Business. When he isn't busy with homework or typesetting and research projects for The Ḥabura, he can be found building his library of Jewish studies or spending time with local Ḥabura members. He currently resides in Miami Beach with his wife, Elisheva.

✦

What is The Ḥabura?

The Ḥabura is an online and global *Bet Midrash* dedicated to studying, teaching, and publishing Torah as a lens through which we view and interact with God's world. This approach is rooted in, but not exclusive to, the classical Sephardi *mesora* that we uphold and cherish.

Since our inception in 2020, we have grown to teach hundreds of international students from across four continents and who work in a variety of professions. We have been honoured to host *Dayanim*, *Rabbanim*, and leading experts from around the world to teach us *Miqra*, *Halakha*, *Talmud*, *Maḥshaba*, and History.

Under the guidance of our *Rosh Bet Midrash*, Rabbi Joseph Dweck, and with the assistance of the S&P Sephardi Community, the Montefiore Endowment, and Dangoor Education, The Ḥabura has been able to utilise the latest technologies to teach and publish authentic, cutting-edge, and relevant Torah-study materials to an unlimited and ever-growing number of Jews, wherever they may live.

For information about our online curriculum, publishing house and more, please visit **www.TheHabura.com.**

✦

THE
ḤABURA

www.TheHabura.com

✦

the SEPHARDI community

Montefiore Endowment

DANGOOR EDUCATION

THE SENIOR RABBI'S OFFICE

Printed in Great Britain
by Amazon

78785057R00150